H a
.Com Business
Plan

S0-AUJ-642

Lethbridge Community College Library

How to Write a .Com Business Plan

The Internet Entrepreneur's Guide to Everything You Need to Know About Business Plans and Financing Options

Joanne Eglash

McGraw-Hill

New York   San Francisco   Washington, D.C.   Auckland   Bogotá
Caracas   Lisbon   London   Madrid   Mexico City   Milan
Montreal   New Delhi   San Juan   Singapore
Sydney   Tokyo   Toronto

Library of Congress Cataloging-in-Publication Data

Eglash, Joanne.
    How to write a .com business plan : the Internet entrepreneur's guide to everything you
need to know about business plans and financing options / by Joanne Eglash.
        p.   cm.
    ISBN 0-07-135753-X
    1. electronic commerce—Management.   2. electronic commerce—Planning.   3. New
business enterprises—Finance.   4. Internet.   I. Title.

HF5548.32.E33   2000
658.4'012—dc21   00-045079

McGraw-Hill

A Division of The McGraw·Hill Companies

Copyright © 2001 by Joanne Eglash. Printed in the United States of America. Except as
permitted under the United States Copyright Act of 1976, no part of this publication
may be reproduced or distributed in any form or by any means, or stored in a data base
or retrieval system, without the prior written permission of the publisher.

1 2 3 4 5 6 7 8 9 0 DOC/DOC   0 9 8 7 6 5 4 3 2 1 0

ISBN 0-07-135753-X

Printed and bound by R.R. Donnelley & Sons Company.

McGraw-Hill books are available at special quantity discounts to use as premiums
and sales promotions, or for use in corporate training programs. For more information,
please write to the Director of Special Sales, Professional Publishing, McGraw-Hill,
Two Penn Plaza, New York, NY 10121-2298. Or contact your local bookstore.

This book is printed on recycled, acid-free paper containing a
minimum of 50% recycled de-inked fiber.

Contents

Acknowledgments and Dedication

My most grateful appreciation to Lisa, without whom this book would never have become a reality: thank you for your support and guidance. I also am grateful to Susan, Nancy, Michelle, and Gillian, editors extraordinaire, all of whom have contributed to this endeavor. Graphic designer and artist M. E. Taylor contributed her skills to my book and her humor to my life; Christine Harmel graciously offered her wisdom and wit from the beginning. To the many entrepreneurs and industry experts who shared their experiences and knowledge, I am deeply appreciative. I also am grateful to the marvelous, magical librarians at the Scotts Valley Library in Santa Cruz County, where I spent many hours investigating topics ranging from vertical portals to cross-border valuation.

I dedicate this book to my mother, who has embraced the Age of the Internet with more enthusiasm (albeit considerably less profit) than Bill Gates.

PART ONE

THE PLAN

1
Introduction

Just a little over five years ago, Amazon.com existed only in its creator's vision. Access to the Internet highway was often a bumpy ride, and the typical retail entrepreneur placed "location, location, location" high on the list of essentials for success.

Welcome to the brave new Webbed World! Amazon.com is viewed as one of the most stellar successes in the Internet sky. Surfing the Web has become just as easy and fast—and in some cases, a heck of a lot more educational, entertaining, and exciting—as TV channel surfing. More and more entrepreneurs these days regard a great domain name as infinitely more valuable than the location of their business.

The Internet has become a force to be reckoned with in the business world—and woe unto you if that force is not with you. Consider the statistics. As reported in the marketing resource Web site eMarketer (emarketer.com), recent researchers have shown that "purchases on the Net are quickly catching up with shopping." One study indicated a more than 40 percent increase from 1998 to 1999 of PCs involved in e-commerce, amounting to 37 million PCs. In addition, eMarketer reported that "the number of computers used to make online purchases jumped 72 percent, which is double the increase of those who went online just to shop."

Pretty impressive.

The pervasive and persuasive power of the Internet literally struck home with me when my mother (until recently, a self-described "computerphobic illiterate") became an Internet addict. It happened so insidiously. In early March, she was debating acquiring a computer "with one of those connections so I can e-mail my cousin, because she got a computer."

By mid-May, Mom was clicking off e-mail messages right and left, in between hopping from a Web site to a newsgroup to a chat room (where she created a new persona for herself, "MomFreud"). And of course she had to check all her favorite shopping sites, to see if they had any specials.

"It's so wonderful! I have the world in my living room," my mother raved. "Not to mention my choice of the most fabulous shopping malls."

I fully expect a candidate for president to run soon on the "An Internet Connection in Every Living Room" ticket.

My mother's experience convinced me: if entrepreneurs snooze, they lose when it comes to the e-commerce game. Dot it with a com.

WHAT CAN THIS BOOK DO FOR YOU?

You've been watching the world of electronic commerce explode in terms of profitability and expansion. Even the smallest dot-com businesses are getting a sizable byte of investors' and venture capitalists' dollars. And you're thinking, "If Mom-and-Pop-dot-com can make it, why can't I?" You can answer that question yourself—by replying to these three key queries.

1. Do You Have a Passion for Your New Enterprise?

It's a wild, wild Internet world out there—which translates, for online entrepreneurs, into long hours. If you relish your new venture and wake up each morning excited about focusing your complete attention on your newbiz-dot-com, you increase the odds of success. You'll enjoy cherishing and nurturing your business—and that devotion will translate into a quality product or service.

2. Do You Have a Support System?

No, we're not talking tech support, customer support, or a house that's been earthquake-reinforced (although if you live in California, that's a good idea). When you're starting a business, you need someone in whom to confide, someone with whom you can share your joys, challenges, and dilemmas. Couple that with the fact that creating an online venture involves minimal human interaction and long hours alone at the keyboard, and it can get mighty lonely. So, whether it's your "significant other," your best friend, and/or your 12 brothers and sisters, it helps to have a friend. I know one new business owner who says, quite seriously, that he would never have succeeded if it had not been for his dog Toto, who "listened faithfully and solemnly to all my trials and tribulations—and regarded a long walk and extra doggy biscuit as the ultimate reward."

3. Are You Confident That This Is What You Want to Do?

Confidence in yourself and your newbiz-dot-com is another way to measure the likelihood of your success. If you believe in yourself and your work—with the self-assurance and faith that the Internet highway is, to misquote Robert Frost, "the road that will make all the difference" in your life—then you're ready to board the e-commerce train! This guide is the ticket for a successful and profitable voyage.

WHY YOU NEED A BUSINESS PLAN

A business plan should be regarded as an absolute essential, whether you're:

- A bright-eyed and bushy-tailed entrepreneur with a GreatIdea-dot-com.
- The owner of a "real-world" business who wants to enter the dot-com domain.
- The proud possessor of a very popular—but currently unprofitable—Web site who is ready to garner more than compliments from your success!

When I told a friend that I was writing this book, she said cheerfully, "Well, I'm starting my own business, but I certainly don't need a plan! I'll be the only employee, and I'll be working from home. And I'm financing it with the haul I took in from trading Internet stocks!"

Hmmm. The product that my friend (let's call her Cheerful Cherie) plans to market is her homemade jam. She hopes to sell it to gourmet stores locally and, via a Web site, to retail customers worldwide. What I gently suggested to Cherie—and what I would advise anyone who wants to start a business without a plan—is that she pretend that, rather than starting a business, she's getting prepared to build a house on her own.

"Would you construct your house without some type of blueprint?" I asked her.

"Of course not," Cherie said indignantly. "I'd need to have a plan to follow. And what if I discovered I couldn't do it on my own? I'd have to hire someone to help, and I'd need a blueprint for that person to follow."

Exactly.

By creating a business plan, you build:

- A résumé that can make or break your ability to secure financing, wow prospective investors, and lure top employees.

- A roadmap for the future, for both you and your colleagues, a way to plan for tomorrow—and the next five years.

- A method for evaluating just how you can most effectively manage your business and market your product or service, and a blueprint for implementing those concepts.

- A way to develop descriptions of your company, your products or services, your financial projections, as well as a method for detailing how you can beat your competition—all of which you should have in place before you begin.

Thus, the answer is: "Yes, Cherie, you need a business plan to build a solid foundation under your dream castle in the air."

WHAT'S IN THIS BOOK

By following the steps detailed in this guide, you can create a plan for a successful and profitable dot-com business. In addition to recommendations and tips for what to include, I offer "red-flag warnings" on what to avoid. For example, there's a Silicon Valley start-up anecdote about a would-be Web entrepreneur with a truly can't-miss idea (this techno-urban legend doesn't reveal what that surefire concept was, of course). He spent a full year researching every aspect of and writing about his business, from creating a mission statement to evaluating his competitors to projecting his financial statistics.

Then our entrepreneur sent in his business plan to the top venture capital firms, confident that he'd procure all the money he needed. He received 100 percent "no-go" replies. Why? Because Mr. Can't-Miss also couldn't spell. He considered grammar something that "elementary school kids gotta study, but why should I care?" His typing ability wouldn't have won any awards either. All those elements, coupled with the fact that he scribbled in some additional notes before xeroxing his proposal on a copier that was low on toner, made for an almost unreadable plan. So, as you'll learn in Chapter 11, on "final flourishes," those so-called little things can mean a lot when it comes to finalizing your plan.

Just one more note before you focus on your business plan. Even if you have an absolutely brilliant idea for a dot-com business that is guaranteed to reap Major Money from the bonanza of opportunity that the Internet presents these days, I recommend that you play "Name That Site." In the online world, the right name can make or break a company.

Take the time to do an informal usability test with your prospective name for your new site. Ask friends, neighbors, the mail carrier, and the dentist what they think of your dot-com name. You want something, such as Make-Money-Over-Night-dot-com, that is guaranteed to attract attention—and investors. Just remember: registering your domain name immediately is a must in these days of "I'll-Pay-You-A-Million-Dollars-For-That-Great-Dot-Com-Name!" If you don't, you run the risk of someone else becoming the master of what was supposed to be your domain.

For more details on choosing and registering a site name, see the Dot-Com Directory later in this book.

SPEAKING OF A DOT-COM DIRECTORY . . .

Part Two of this book includes your very own Dot-Com Directory. In it, you'll find information about topics ranging from how to research your target market to where to locate venture capital firms. Although most of the recommendations are online (as only befits an Internet entrepreneur's book), I've also included some suggestions for a little light reading. Keeping up with industry and business publications will help you stay on top of market trends. Not to mention that it's one of the best ways of tracking just what your competition is up to, and learning about that new kid on the Internet block!

A PICTURE'S WORTH 1000 WORDS

Just as a picture's worth 1000 words, a relevant example can be more helpful than 1000 pages of conceptual chatter. Which brings us to two sites that I've concocted to illustrate my points throughout this book: Grrlbiz.com and Turnip-Chips.com.

Grrlbiz.com is designed to encourage girls and young women to become entrepreneurs and to educate them about finance and the business world. It will utilize experts in various areas as columnists and "chat room" experts, in addition to bringing in the services of venture capital firms, banks, women's groups, the federal government's small business and businesswomen sections, and existing groups such as Junior Achievement.

Turnip-Chips.com, in contrast, markets an imaginary product that looks and tastes like potato chips. It is low-calorie, seasoned with antioxidants and other health and longevity ingredients, and a winner in a variety of taste tests throughout the nation. In addition, Turnip-Chips.com's manufacturing features a gigantic turnip slicer and outdoor gizmo that will bake the turnip slices with the power of the sun.

Throughout this guide, I'll use these two sites as case studies to help you understand how to implement the information.

NOW, A WORD (OR TWO, OR THREE . . .) ABOUT VENTURE CAPITAL FIRMS

Any Internet entrepreneurs out there who haven't heard the buzz about the money available from venture capital firms? Raise your hand. Hmmm. That's what I thought. The increase in funding from venture capital firms has garnered enormous publicity lately. And yes, it's true: these folks have big bucks to invest in prospective companies. But remember: before they'll show you the money, honey, they want reassurance that you have a profitable plan that will succeed.

Once you get the plan, well, you've also probably heard or read the reports of Ordinary Joes and Janes making a million overnight.

Is it fiction? No. The statistics and stories are indeed impressive—and encouraging. For example, the *San Francisco Chronicle* reported that venture capital financing into Internet companies in the quarter ended March 1999 increased nearly a third more than the previous quarter, totaling $2.1 billion. And ZDNet recently cited forecasts showing that, by 2003, e-commerce internationally could generate $3.2 trillion.

Now, aren't you glad that you decided to invest in a book that will guide you to a business plan appealing to those venture angels out there?!

WHY CW IS NOW WC—AND HOW I KNOW

Used to be that you could read a book or two on writing a business plan, grab yourself one of those prettily packaged, create-your-own-business-plan-in-a-day software programs, and voilà! You had a business plan fit for a blue-suited banker. It probably ranged from 100 to 200 pages, and contained an extensive executive summary, because Conventional Wisdom (CW) said that was how long it should be and that the exec summary section was guaranteed to be the most important.

Then e-commerce turned CW upside down and inside out. Which is why, in addition to studying all those business plan books, I turned to the key players who could clue me in: the Web Connoisseurs (WC). My mavens ranged from Guy Kawasaki, founder of Garage.com and former Apple Computer evangelist, to Brad Garlinghouse, a general partner with @Ventures, the venture capital arm of CMGI, to a variety of Internet entrepreneurs. In general, recommendations for the length of a business plan and views on the most important sections differed considerably from CW.

Brad Garlinghouse, for example, notes that @Ventures receives more than 1000 business plans each month. He recommends that you make your business plan "short, concise, and to the point. Over 25 pages is too much."

There are three areas in a business plan to which he gives "the most attention. And frankly, these are the first areas I read. If I don't make it past these, I never see the rest: (1) team—the most important factor of success; (2) market opportunity—how large the business opportunity is; and (3) competition—who the existing players are. *Everyone* has competitors, and failure to acknowledge this is a big mistake. Moreover, failure to identify some obvious competitors indicates lack of awareness and understanding of the market."

Brad also views domain names as "very important. They need to be short and catchy. It's not a coincidence that some of the most successful Web sites (and public companies) are short words (e.g., Yahoo, Excite, eBay, Amazon). We have spent amazing sums of money acquiring the 'right' domain name. Furniture.com is one example. Carparts.com is another. We're actively buying domains right now for other companies."

Guy Kawasaki of Garage.com warns about assuming that citing millions of statistics will automatically result in millions of investors' dollars. "Every plan we see says that 'IDC predicts that by 2005 this market will be $20 billion,'" he says. "These external verifications are meaningless. The idea has to make inherent sense. No analyst's prediction can overcome an idea that doesn't make sense."

I also asked Guy about the value that he places upon a Web site's domain name, noting how many in existing sites have decided to play the name change game (Computer Literacy, for example, recently changed its site name to Fatbrain.com). "If the company had a killer domain, it would help," agrees Guy. "For example, Loans.com, Car.com, Clothes.com, or Garage.com. But a mediocre domain isn't a deal breaker." And he contends that "no business plan should be more than 20 pages. So the process is to send a short exec summary to see if there's interest. If there is, then meet and leave a 20-page plan."

Entrepreneur Elizabeth Slocum, the founder of e-consults.com, says that she "firmly" believes in the power of business plans. "I think the business plan is a great tool or roadmap for the entrepreneur. It gives one direction and an ability to stay on track. It also gives one realistic goals to aim for. Business plans are a necessity for obtaining funding." Elizabeth's company "addresses the how-to of e-business by defining a company's online strategic role and assisting in the design, deployment, and marketing of successful e-business initiatives."

As she reflects on her experience in becoming an Internet entrepreneur, Elizabeth says, "I love my life. I love what I have been able to accomplish in a short amount of time. I have zero regrets and would do this again in a heartbeat." She offers this advice for would-be dot-com entrepreneurs: "Love what you do and make it your passion, because you spend *so much* time at it. There are so many people who want to start a company to chase the IPO (Initial Public Offering) gravy train, but they have no knowledge of the business. Know how much money it truly takes, to build a brand—the Amazons of the world did not come cheap. Another piece of advice is not to let rejection deter you. If you really want it, you can make it happen. Of course there is a time to let certain things go, but I don't know how many times people have told me, 'Wow—how can you start your own business? It will never work.'"

Throughout this book, I've included this type of information and direct quotations from those immediately involved in the exciting, ever-changing world of e-commerce. In other words: people actively engaged in a realm that you are about to explore. So consider this book your travel guide to that brave new world. And now, without further ado: upward and onward on the Internet ramp!

2
Executive Summary

If Yogi Berra were asked to write an executive summary, he would probably pause, sigh, and reflect, "But what if I write it and no executives read it? It's dejà vu all over again!"

Ouch.

But seriously, folks. I recommend that you skip the Yogi Berra jokes, references to your children (unless you are selling a product or service for kids), and other potential wince-isms in your executive summary. Remember: many prospective investors use the summary as a way to decide whether your plan is worth additional time—and you don't want to make them groan or feel sick on the second page. If you must be cute, save it for your appendix. (See Chapter 11 for details.)

So, now that we've set aside the bad jokes (at least for the moment), let's look at the facts. Want some incentive for writing a dynamic executive summary? Here's the reality: an outstanding executive summary is an absolutely essential element in winning investment dollars from venture capital, venture catalyst, and/or individual investor "angels"

Tip: One way to regard the executive summary is to consider how people select books to purchase. They're standing in a bookstore, browsing through the shelves. First they notice a catchy title (in this case, the name of your business, which will appear on your cover and title page). Then they turn over the book and read the capsule description on the back cover. If that tempts them, they leaf through the table of contents and book itself. The executive summary is your description of your brilliant plan—and you know you want to do justice to it.

---

for your lightbulb lollipalooza of an idea. These folks' desks are piled to the ceiling with BrightBusinessPlans-dot-coms. And they're going to read your executive summary first. If it doesn't whet their appetite for more, you can bid a fond farewell to all your hard work!

TWO COMMON APPROACHES—PLUS HERE'S MY VERSION

There are two frequently used methods for writing an executive summary:

- The Write It First School of Thought, which is based on the theory that you can then use this summary as an outline for the rest of your business plan.
- The Write It Last Philosophy, which is based on the theory that you can combine sections from the preceding parts of your plan to use in the executive summary.

I recommend a third method. Do a quick-and-dirty draft at the onset. Then, during your "final flourishes" (as outlined in Chapter 11), you can smooth the rough edges, add and modify as needed, and voilà! You have an executive summary fit for the grandest of poohbah executives.

What does an executive summary contain? The summary provides the reader with an overview of:

- The company mission statement and company description
- The management
- The competition
- The market and your customer
- Your product and/or service
- Marketing and sales
- Operations
- Financial projections and plans

It is essential to prepare this section with care. Remember: many of your readers will glance through the summary first. If it seems like a winner, they'll continue. If not, they will simply move onto the next business plan.

One common mistake is to overwrite the executive summary, cramming in every iota of information. This everything-but-the-kitchen-sink approach might seem like the way to impress your readers.

Wrong. Bankers, venture capital firms, individual investors—all these folks have one trait in common: they value their time. You should too. So, keep your executive summary succinct and clear. Your goal is to capture your readers' attention, not drown it.

Because you are creating a business plan for an Internet business, you must also demonstrate how you will get site traffic on an ongoing basis (and why they'll keep comin' back). What I'm referring to here is the "stickiness" factor. Before you rush off to purchase a virtual version of glue, here's what I mean by stickiness. It's the features that make visitors linger at your Web site and give them reason to return time after time—in a nutshell, the qualities of your site that increase both new and return visitors.

Addressing this element helps present your site as a winning proposition for investors. And remember: if investors buy the snapshot of your vision, they'll continue. For example, in the executive summary for Grrlbiz.com, I would note our plans to offer free e-mail accounts (one way to guarantee that visitors will return: they need to check, compose, and manage their free Grrlbiz.com e-mail accounts); changing content, such as columns by experts; community involvement and opportunities for interaction, such as chats and discussion boards; and contests. But remember: this is just a first draft. Don't let the importance of your executive summary overwhelm you so much that you belabor it. Look at it as an opportunity to capture all your ideas in just a few pages.

If you can't complete all the sections (such as the financial details), don't worry. The "final flourishes" chapter is when we'll fill in all the blanks! So, although you will need to revise this section after the other chapters are finished, you'll benefit and save time later by creating this draft as a reference point.

I CANNOT TELL A LIE

Here's something to remember as you write your summary and throughout your business plan preparation: tell the truth. Just as in creating a résumé, you may be tempted to exaggerate a trifle, to stretch the facts into a form that sounds more impressive. Don't give into temptation! Consider the possibly disastrous consequences.

Here's a case in point. During the Microsoft/Netscape court testimony, Microsoft charged that statements made by Netscape chief executive James Barksdale contrasted with statistics that Netscape gave bankers when America Online was evaluating whether to purchase Netscape. Ouch. Journalists had a field day, writing headlines such as "Netscape Fibs?" and other not-exactly-good-for-PR blurbs.

GUIDELINES

Note that the following guidelines are just that: guidelines, not rules cast in stone. There is no one-size-fits-all, cookie cutter of a business plan that can apply to EveryBiz-dot-com. Adapt these recommendations to your own situation:

- Keep your executive summary limited to two pages—three if you include a chart, graph, or other illustration.
- Take time to craft the mission statement and company description, as detailed later in this chapter.
- Don't underestimate the importance of your management team: prospective investors will want to know that you have a solid management organization in place.
- Describe your competition. (If you have not yet completed this research, do a quick draft now, spend time following the guidelines in the competition chapter, and finalize this section later.) Point out why you'll be the winner. You need to show that you've planned your attack thoroughly.
- Describe your customer and the market that you are targeting, demonstrating that you know your customer and particular marketing area.
- Describe your product or service. What needs are you fulfilling by offering that item? Make it clear just why someone will want to purchase what you've got to offer.
- What are your marketing and sales plans? Remember: those investors and lenders (yes, even your mom and dad) want to know that they'll

get more than the glow of giving from their investment, and an outstanding marketing and sales program can make the difference between a boom and a bust, especially in "Internet time."

- Demonstrate that you have thought through the operations portion of your e-biz (particularly important if you are doing any type of manufacturing and/or shipping).

- Describe the type of financing you have—and how much more you will need. It's critical to an investor's decision as to whether to pass or sign: just what do you want?

With those guidelines in mind, let's start.

YOUR MISSION, SHOULD YOU CHOOSE TO ACCEPT IT, AND COMPANY DESCRIPTION

Mission Statement

What is your goal or purpose—your *raison d'être*, or reason for being? Perhaps it is to build the world's greatest widget and sell it on the Internet. Or maybe you want to help isolated senior citizens by offering them an online support system.

Using Grrlbiz.com as an example, here's my quick-and-dirty concept: Grrlbiz.com seeks to encourage girls and young women to become entrepreneurs and to educate them about finance and the business world.

Company Description

What makes your company unique? How will it grow? And what factors will make it profitable? You need to make your strategies and objectives clear.

Because you are writing a dot-com business plan, it's important to include your site name in this section. Why? Because an easily remembered and instantly recognizable moniker makes you, literally, the master of your domain. For example, if you see the site name Drugstore.com, you instantly know what to expect.

Also included in the description should be your company's structure, history, staff and management, and products and services in brief.

And show what will make your site special, one to which consumers will return. You'll want to focus on the "stickiness" factor of your site, as noted above.

If you have already started your business, include its history.

Grrlbiz.com's company description would emphasize the various ways in which the site can attract girls and young women and educate them about business, finance, and, in particular, entrepreneurship. In addition to staff experts, Grrlbiz.com would draw on existing resources by utilizing the services of venture capital firms, banks, women's groups, the federal government's small business and businesswomen sections, and existing groups such as Junior Achievement. Planned features include chat rooms, with scheduled talks with and by experts in different areas, free e-mail, bulletin boards, and other forums to interact with Grrlbiz.com's community and provide growth.

THE MANAGEMENT

In the management section, it is important to describe members of the management team and their qualifications. Focus on their expertise in relevant areas. You should include their names, titles, and responsibilities. If you plan to use consultants and have already selected them, include this information as well. Depending on the nature of your business and structure, you may also want to include a summary of how you will recruit employees, with reference, if appropriate, to an organizational chart. For example, suppose that you're starting a business for the year 3000, and it's well-known that Y3K experts are in short supply and high demand—as well as notorious for requiring micromanagers to oversee them. Specifics on how you'd attract these critical personnel and manage them would be essential reading for potential investors. For example, you could note that you are aware of just how hot such professionals are these days, and that you have studied both the difficulty in recruiting them and the special "perks" that attract and retain them. Then describe your plans to lure the best. Free doggie day care? A basketball court, free video games, and a "help yourself" policy on a refrigerator full of ice cream bars, bagels, and Yoo-hoos? Clarify your plans and impress your readers with how foresighted you are.

Grrlbiz.com's management details would need to include information on key managers such as the content director, who should be accustomed to writing about girls and young women, with an understanding of their needs and interests.

THE COMPETITION

Unless you've discovered a niche market so undisputedly unique that no competitors exist on the face of this planet (and these days, better make that the universe), you must show that you know your competition—and that your dot-com biz is the best dot-com biz in the galaxy.

This section definitely requires (1) research: to sleuth out your potential competitors, and (2) analysis: to evaluate just why you can be in the best of category. Otherwise, that wonderful Pogo quote, "We have seen the enemy and he is us," will be all too true. In Grrlbiz.com's competitive section, for example, I would make it clear that I've analyzed all the competitors—and there are, unfortunately, many. After evaluating every company from iVillage.com to Grrl.com to Women.com, I can truthfully write, however, that I could not locate a competitor that focuses on the specific issues that Grrlbiz.com does. I would also emphasize the "stickability" factor of the "community" aspect of the site, with the bulletin boards and chat rooms.

> **Red-Flag Warning:** It's a major mistake to airily say, "Oh, I'm unique! I don't have any real competition." Such statements will cause your readers to raise their eyebrows, smile pityingly at your naiveté, and move on to the next Joe's or Jane's business plan. So, spend time researching not only your prospective clients and market, but just who and what you're up against.

THE MARKET AND YOUR CUSTOMER

In the market and customer section, you will need to show that you understand the market that you are serving. It should be evident to your readers that you have researched your prospective customer or client and the current market trends in that segment. You need to demonstrate that your product or service is precisely what your profile customer or client needs and wants—and will buy.

The market and customer section for Turnip-Chips.com would discuss the profile of the target audience (both men and women who are health-conscious and/or weight-conscious and want to enjoy a virtuous way to snack on delicious foods). It would make the point that as baby boomers age, they increasingly pay attention to ways to improve their physical well-being. Because Turnip Chips are low-calorie, with more "munch crunch" and taste than the average chip, they will attract the weight-conscious consumer. And, since they have been demonstrated to reduce the risk of cancer and health disease and increase memory as well, Turnip Chips are a guaranteed best-seller among baby boomers.

Tip: Consider this quote from Stanley Marcus, Neiman Marcus' "chair emeritus": "It's a question of how you get the merchandise you're infatuated with into the hands of the people you like." (Source: *Wired* magazine, March 1999.)

See the Dot-Com Directory in Part Two for help with locating demographics and statistics for this information.

PRODUCTS AND SERVICES

Before you even start drafting the product or service section, make sure that you understand your prospective customer or client. "Know thyself" is excellent advice—and, if you're in business, I recommend that you also seek to "understand thy customer's needs and expectations."

In this section, make it clear precisely what it is that you are offering—and how that product and/or service will attract your target customer. Is it something that customers need? That they want? That will get them to return to your site to see what else you have for sale? What's unique about it?

In the case of Turnip Chips, this section would include specific data from the tests and analyses that were run, comparing them against like products to demonstrate that no snack food can beat Turnip Chips in its unique low-calorie, health-improving, good-taste ratings.

Need an example?

Amazon.com is one of the top e-commerce success stories. Why? Because of emphasis on providing the customer with what he or she wants: a quick way to browse and buy products at a more than competitive price. (The current focus is on books, although the sky's apparently the limit as far as the site's founders are concerned. I expect to be able to purchase ownership of a shooting star there any day now.) In addition, clever customer-focused features such as customer reviews, optional newsletters, and free electronic greeting cards make it an experience that browsers and buyers want to repeat. Just sample the attention given to customers in buying a book, returning it, and sending customer service a question. Instant responses! The result? Customer satisfaction with both the product and the service.

MARKETING AND SALES

How do you plan to market your product? What will you do for public relations? You can have the best product or service in the world—but if there's no buzz, there's no business. Some of the keys to this area are:

- Market research: analyzing and evaluating the target sector and profiling your customer.
- Focus groups: gathering and using feedback from potential customers and/or clients.
- Developing synergy between your marketing and sales teams, so that the information gathered by the marketing group is clearly conveyed to the sales department. (You can have a terrific marketing story and press releases—but if the sales and customer service troops don't get clued into the big picture, you'll win a tiny battle but lose the war.)

Thus, for Turnip-Chips.com, marketing and sales methods would include free samples of Turnip Chips at health clubs and fitness spas across the country, product demonstrators with literature and free samples in grocery stores and health stores nationwide, sales pitches to physicians, press releases and samples to health and fitness magazine editors and TV show producers, and related rollouts. In addition, the Web site would be listed in search engines, directories, and industry publications. See the Dot-Com Directory for more details.

OPERATIONS

Part of the magic for some Internet entrepreneurs is the opportunity to run the entire operation from home. If you plan to operate from the comforts of your living room, don't attempt to hide that fact. Emphasize it and use it to your advantage by pointing to the cost savings and the ability to be flexible and available as needed 24 hours a day.

If you do plan to have additional space allocated, however, specify its location, size, and use. For example, Turnip-Chips.com would need to have storage space available for the various products, along with a manufacturing, packaging, and delivery mechanism.

FINANCIAL PROJECTIONS AND PLANS

The finance section should include an estimate of the targeted market's potential. Calculate the figures for each quarter of the first five years (two at a minimum). You also should include what funds you have now—a loan from your father-in-law, money borrowed from a 401(k) plan at your "day job," and so forth—and what funds you estimate you will need.

Questions answered in this section should be:

- How will you use your funds?
- At what rate can they be repaid?
- What profit can investors hope to make?

> **Tip:** This area is one in which you may want to hire an expert. Be honest with yourself. If crunching numbers and analyzing forecasts is not your bailiwick, it will be worth your investment to seek a consultant's services.

In the case of Grrlbiz.com, I would seek references from others in my area and hire a financial whiz who could help build that foundation under my castle-in-the-air dot-com dreams.

Checklist

To ensure that you've incorporated all the initial elements in your final executive summary, check off each item on this list of executive summary sections:

☐ The company mission statement and company description
☐ The management
☐ The competition
☐ The market and your customer
☐ Your product and/or service
☐ Marketing and sales
☐ Operations
☐ Financial projections and plans

3

Mission Statement and Company Description

Although a mission statement and a company description are separate concepts, they often are combined in a business plan. Why? Because your mission statement expresses your philosophy, motivation, and goals with regard to your business. Your company description, in contrast, presents your idea and concept. They are equally important, as you'll see in this chapter.

CRAFTING YOUR MISSION STATEMENT

Your mission statement will be studied not only by investors but by both current and prospective employees and the public. Thus, crafting it carefully and thoughtfully will more than pay off in the long run.

Most companies display their mission statements on their Web sites; some have their mission statements incorporated into their logos, ads, and stationery. To view some different types of mission statements, you may want to visit a variety of Web sites and read some annual reports from different companies, particularly those in the same category (e.g., business to business, retail).

The U.S. Department of Agriculture, for example, states that its mission is to "enhance the quality of life for the American people" by:

- Supporting production of agriculture.

- Ensuring a safe, affordable, nutritious, and accessible food supply.

- Caring for agricultural, forest, and range lands supporting sound development of rural communities.

- Providing economic opportunities for farm and rural residents.
- Expanding global markets for agricultural and forest products and services.
- Working to reduce hunger in America and throughout the world.

Contrast this vision with that of the U.S. Department of Commerce. Its mission is to promote "job creation, economic growth, sustainable development, and improved living standards for all Americans by working in partnership with business, universities, communities, and workers." To this end the DOC seeks to:

- Build for the future and promote U.S. competitiveness in the global marketplace by strengthening and safeguarding the nation's economic infrastructure.
- Keep America competitive with cutting-edge science and technology and an unrivaled information base.
- Provide effective management and stewardship of the nation's resources and assets to ensure sustainable economic opportunities.

Although both mission statements are rather lengthy, they illustrate the ways in which this section of the business plan can showcase your personal dream and company vision in a way that is, as much as possible, unique to your dot-com.

TRY A BRAINSTORM BREAK

One way to create a mission statement is by brainstorming. You can brainstorm alone or in a group. And whether you work alone or with others, focus first on producing as many ideas and thoughts as possible. Don't judge or dismiss an idea, whether it is yours or a colleague's. Just write down every and any concept and suggestion.

After you've unleashed all your wild and woolly notions, write them on a chalkboard and play with them. Combine and try out different phrases. Say them out loud. If you are working in a group, maintain the guideline of accepting, not rejecting, all suggestions. After all the suggestions have been noted, take a break.

The final refinement of your mission statement, whether you're working alone or with a group, may not be achieved immediately. Give yourself time to contemplate a few different ideas—to try "living" with them—before you finalize your mission statement. And remember: your mission statement need not and should not be regarded as forever final. Depending on changes in your business, trends, and any unexpected shifts in your customer base, you may want to modify your mission statement at some point in your dot-com's growth.

For example, suppose that the Turnip-Chips.com Web site included a fitness and nutrition section, with "virtual coaches" specializing in personal fitness training and diet and nutrition counseling. The initial brainstorming session might result in these key terms: turnips, weight loss, energy, longevity, long life, health, fitness, exercise, nutrition, diet, weight loss, coach, encourage, endorphins, trim, sleek, slim, muscular, fun, energize. And the final mission statement might be: "Enjoy improved health and a longer life by snacking on a taste winner, Turnip Chips! Take advantage of our expert fitness and nutrition counseling to increase your health even more."

Suppose, however, that the nutrition counseling option fails to attract customers—and that virtual personal fitness coaching is highly successful? Moreover, what if surveys reveal that 97 percent of customers purchase Turnip Chips because they want to lose weight, and they could care less about the other benefits? The company's revised mission statement could be: "Enjoy easy weight loss and improved health by snacking on low-calorie, delicious Turnip Chips! Energize and thrive with our unique personalized fitness training!"

In the same way, suppose that Grrlbiz.com had a section in which young women and girls could purchase a product at wholesale, and then resell it, thus teaching them about entrepreneurism. This product and area could be called the Grrl's Java Café. Products would include imported coffee beans packaged with special mugs and accessories. For example, a Down Home Blend would be accompanied by sturdy mugs and just-baked doughnuts; a Cinnamon Brew package of coffee beans would come with mugs decorated with spice graphics and cinnamon sticks. Those young entrepreneurs' mission statement could be "Savor the full bean experience!"

COMPANY DESCRIPTION

Although your mission statement may include generalities, your company description should be as specific as possible. If you're not sure where to start, begin by drafting an elevator pitch. After you've polished that pitch, utilize it in your executive summary.

Not familiar with an "elevator pitch"? I first heard the term not in Silicon Valley, but in the Valley of Valley Girls, Los Angeles. My would-be actress friends would ask to try out their elevator pitches on me. Here's how one of them explained it: "Pretend that you work at a major talent agency or film studio. You step into the elevator on the twenty-fourth floor of the building. I'm the only other occupant. As the elevator starts to move, you yawn and casually ask, 'Know what the weather's like outside?'

"I grab my chance—I figure I've got about 20 to 30 seconds. 'Yes,' I say. 'I just came into the building from an audition in the Valley for a sitcom. I'm taking the updates to my portfolio to my agent.'"

Shazam! There's the entrance line into this actress's elevator pitch.

The keys to creating your elevator pitch include:

- Keep it short and succinct.
- Imagine that your reader knows nothing about your background (in other words, don't assume that he or she has studied your executive summary thoroughly—perhaps the reader only glanced at it, saw something intriguing, and moved onto this section).
- Envision yourself literally stepping onto an elevator and discovering a venture angel standing there looking bored—what would you say to capture his or her attention?

Just how important is this section? Well, according to Guy Kawasaki, CEO and chairman of Garage.com, potential investors spend the most time reading your "elevator pitch" when they review your business plan. The former chief evangelist of Apple Computer, Kawasaki has started two software companies and served as a venture "angel" for three other companies.

A note about your site's name. Although you may be still evaluating names in an attempt to come up with a truly memorable and unique moniker, including it in your business plan is generally regarded as important. If you omit it, prospective investors may be left wondering if you're not as Internet-savvy as you should be. So, if you've been delaying creating and registering a site, check out the Dot-Com Directory for help—and get that name registered now! It's just like the Wild, Wild West—the best dot-com campsites are going fast!

Don't assume that you need to come up with an instantly recognizable domain name. According to Kawasaki, "If the company had a killer domain, it would help. For example, Loans.com, Car.com, Clothes.com, or Garage.com. But a mediocre domain isn't a deal breaker." Consider, for example, such domain names as Google and Oxygen. Neither popular site name instantly tells you what it offers—but both are growing in terms of their business strength and number of visitors.

In addition to that quick "elevator pitch" overview, your company description may include some or all of the following, depending on such factors as the size and history of your company. (Much of this information can be summarized from other sections, such as the product or service section and market section of your plan.)

- Staff and management. So who's running this dot-com biz anyway? Do you have plans to hire enough employees, or are you big on upper management and hazy about whom else you need? Think about it—and then clarify those issues here, referring readers to the management section for details.

- Products and/or services in brief. What are you selling and how are you selling it?

- The market you are serving. What niche have you targeted? Who are your prospective customers and/or clients? What is the future of this niche? For example, if you've invested a lot of time in creating a site to celebrate the year 2001, what happens to your market in the year 2002? If you can find relevant statistics that apply specifically to your plan, cite them; however, it is better to avoid the numbers game rather than clutter up your plan with irrelevant figures. (See the section on statistics below for more about this point.)

- The reason your business is unique. What will make your Web site special, one to which consumers will return? Focus on the "stickiness" factor—the features that make visitors linger at your Web site—and give them reason to return time after time.

- Your site name.

- Your company's structure.

- Your company's history, including profits and losses. If your history consists only of creating and registering your site name, skip this section. Faking it is not advisable!

- Your plans for selling and marketing. Be sure to include information about customer service and, if applicable, technical support or "help desk" plans.

As an example, here is Grrlbiz.com's company description:

Grrlbiz.com will create a unique niche: a Web site that is designed specifically to educate girls and young women about business, finance, and, in particular, entrepreneurship. In addition to staff experts, Grrlbiz.com will utilize the services of venture capital firms, banks, women's groups, the federal government's small business and businesswomen sections, and existing groups such as Junior Achievement.

Features will include chat rooms with scheduled talks by experts in different areas, free e-mail, bulletin boards, and other forums to interact with Grrlbiz.com's community and provide growth. All messages to customer service and the company will be responded to promptly.

Tip: Ka-ching! What's that ringing? It's the sound of virtual cash registers clanging all over Internetland. And one secret to making the sound of money ring on your site is customer service. Quality service keeps 'em comin' back. Anyone who underestimates the importance of that art will learn that lesson the hard way when the profits and losses get toted up. Consider the success of Disneyland: those smiling, helpful employees are legendary. So be sure to note your awareness of the importance of customer service in your business description.

USING STATISTICS IN THE RIGHT WAY

Some entrepreneurs fall in love with what they see as the power of statistics, sprinkling numbers and figures all over their company description. Well, while you may love doughnuts that are drowning in powdered sugar, don't think that you can sweeten your plan with an excess of stats.

You can do your plan more harm than good if you attempt to create claims for your research that are not true, exaggerate the research's implications, make only a token attempt at research, and/or fail to show precisely how those statistics apply to your company.

Let's use Grrlbiz.com as an example. Since Grrlbiz.com's target audience consists of girls and young women, I would research the market for that sector. Now suppose that I came across a statistic showing that more than 6 million teenagers actively used the Internet in 1998, and that 26 percent of them made an online purchase during that year, according to eMarketer, a New York-based research firm.

Suppose I then use those statistics in my business description, adding the following: "These statistics prove that Grrlbiz.com is guaranteed to be more successful than Amazon.com, since the number of Internet users is constantly growing and more and more women are going online." In this case, I'd be playing a very dangerous game. Unless the investor is a complete novice, he or she will immediately (1) question why the latest statistics (i.e., for 2000) were not used, (2) note that the specifics regarding female teenagers and the exact statistics for Internet users and women in general were not provided, and (3) probably laugh at my claim that I've thus proved that Grrlbiz.com will be a greater success story than Amazon.com.

If you want to use statistics, research them thoroughly and make sure that your conclusions are clearly and logically drawn. Check out the Dot-Com Directory in Part Two for sources on researching these types of statistics and marketing information.

Checklist

Use this checklist to help you finalize your business philosophy and concept:

☐ *Mission statement.* Make sure that your mission statement captures your vision for your company. Compare it with the mission statements of your competition. Does it stand out in the dot-com crowd? Is it unique, showcasing the central and key features and goals of your e-biz?

☐ *Company description.* Imagine that you're an investor, with little time and patience for lengthy documents. Focus on the first sentence only of your description. Does it portray the nature of your e-biz and what makes it unique? After you've polished that statement, make sure that you've included relevant information that, while succinct, illustrates the key strengths of your company. For example, you may want to include the size and any company history, staff and management experience, a brief overview of your products and/or services, your target market, and any positive statistics, selling and marketing plans, and unique qualities.

4
The Management

When asked what elements of an executive summary or business plan they examine first, the investors whom I interviewed differed in some areas. But they almost unanimously pointed to one section: management.

The Mayfield Fund, a Menlo Park-based venture capital partnership, includes among its key players general partner Kevin A. Fong. Commenting on Mayfield's positioning in the venture capital industry, Fong noted, "Mayfield is an early-stage firm. We like to invest early in a company's development, work side by side with the management, and help them take it from concept to product to IPO. It's a highly collaborative and participatory process, and we bring a lot of specialized industry experience to the table. Traditionally, we've invested in technology and product innovation, but in today's world, we are also focusing a lot on business model innovation."

Asked about the importance of the management team, Fong responded, "The management team is the most important element. It defines what markets you are in and your ability to execute. In entrepreneurs, we look for people with vision and a drive to see the world in their vision, and the energy and determination to lead a team of people to make their vision a reality."

In addition, the Mayfield Fund seeks management teams composed of individuals who "listen, who take advice and counsel from their board and partners—people who want to collaborate to reach their objectives." And Fong feels that there are, in essence, "two types of innovators—entrepreneurs, who like to collaborate, and proprietors, who want to do things their own way. We prefer to work with the former, people who want to work with others to achieve their vision."

NAME THAT MANAGER

As Fong's views illustrate, it is critical that you detail and define your own management background and visions as well as those of your management team. Although the résumés of the key founders and management should be included in the appendix of your business plan, you must be as specific as possible in this section. Investors are busy folks, and they may only glance, if that, at your appendix. Be complete and concise as you list the qualities that your managers possess.

Here's some advice from an expert. Marian Banker is president of Prime Strategies, which offers coaching, consulting, and training in business leadership. "The management team for a Web-based business should possess the same comprehensive and well-rounded attributes as in any other business," notes Banker. "Financial, promotion, sales, and leadership are specific skills required to support and build any business. An Internet business also needs technical and information management skills with heavy experience on the Internet. Team members can be part of the organization or they can be brought in on a contract basis. If your core team doesn't have all the skills needed, it may be better to contract for them on the short term with an option to become a member once skills are proven and it's determined that the chemistry works."

If you choose to use consultants or contractors as key members of your management team, you should list their qualifications in your management section as well. In addition to the skills listed above, Banker recommends that you seek individuals who "are project-oriented, because the nature of Web business tends to be project to project. Web-based teams often operate from disparate locations, so the ability to communicate clearly (especially in writing) is important," adds this business expert.

What type of experience should your management team have? "You'll want someone with Internet marketing experience," Banker says, "either on the team or as a consultant, because marketing a Web business is unique and the body of knowledge changes rapidly."

If you do choose to use contractors or consultants, Banker has a warning for you: "Keep in mind that Web time is highly accelerated. The technology and techniques are evolving much more rapidly than in any other form of business. Whatever your plan, keep it flexible. Try to think a couple of years into the future, but don't lock yourself into expensive technology or contracts that may lose value in a short time."

And don't neglect to do an organizational chart, which you also can include in your appendix. In Banker's words: "Delineate a clear working relationship between team members with areas of responsibility clearly defined. Each team member should set goals for his or her area of responsibility. Then hold regular team meetings for a status check. Common mistakes I've seen include professionally or technically competent entrepreneurs trying to run a Web business without putting together a team to round out the management skills needed to run the business. All may go fine for a while, but eventually things get out of control and the entrepreneur has no clue about what action to take."

Options for putting together the right management team vary. Founder of successful Dietsite.com (see Figure 4-1), Traci Van Der Vorste-Kaufman is a registered dietitian. Although her expertise was clearly

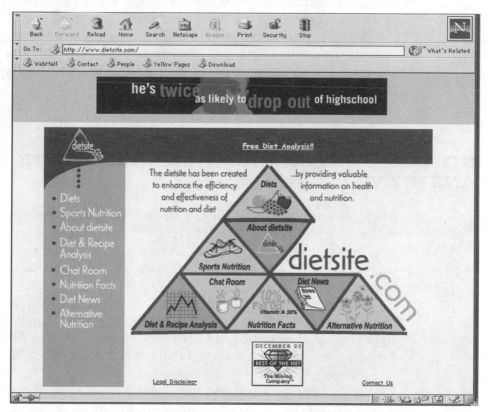

Figure 4-1. There's gold in them thar sites—if you can follow the founder of Dietsite.com's advice and "always produce and maintain the best product."

critical in bringing about the site's success, she knew that she needed to get the advice of experts in other areas crucial to Web business.

"Like many small start-ups, we managed the company with a small management team," recalls Traci. "People perceive Web companies by the quality of the experience they have online. Dietsite was a two-person show with plenty of consultants and brokers who aided in our success. Unlike most Internet companies, Dietsite was earning a profit almost immediately. The thought of recruiting was always on our mind; however, the costs to get top-flight talent were out of our reach. We were left with two options. The first was to get venture capital and give up equity and control. The second was to partner with a vendor who shared our interests in producing exceptional patient content. We chose the latter and agreed to be acquired by IDX Systems Corporation, a leading supplier of health care automation."

This method definitely worked for Traci. "Dietsite started as a small enterprise with modest expectations and blossomed into a heavily visited nutrition portal with millions of visitors worth millions of dollars. This type of growth and impact can only be possible on the Internet. To stay competitive in this business you must always produce and maintain the best product."

And to be the best, management is key.

DO YOU SUFFER FROM ORGANIZATION ANXIETY?

There's something about the traditional "organizational chart" that can make even the most alert entrepreneur start to yawn. However, before you decide to skip this section, consider an important point: creating such a structure can help you evaluate just what functions each management team member fills.

For example, suppose that I offer my friend Jane Dough the position of chief financial officer (CFO) of Grrlbiz.com. Ms. Dough also happens to be a whiz at recruiting, and has more than a decade of experience in human resources. So, although Jane wants the CFO title ("That rocks!"), she agrees to lead the human resources and recruiting effort as well. Clarifying her roles on an organizational chart can help pinpoint how she will complement the other members of my team, and assist in demonstrating our collaborative methodology.

If an individual's educational background is applicable to the functions she or he will perform, include that as well. Suppose that I select Mary Dotcom as my head of Marketing and Sales. My description of Mary would include the following:

> Mary Dotcom will manage the advertising, promotion, marketing, and sales functions of Grrlbiz.com. She brings to the position of executive vice president more than two decades of experience.
>
> After earning her Ph.D. in management from Harvard University, Mary started her own company, MyBaby, which produced a highly popular line of clothes for infants and toddlers. After taking her company public, Mary chose to accept an offer to become director of sales and marketing at the Universe's-Largest-Internet-Service-Provider-dot-com. She became well known in her field for her strong communication skills, and her marketing group won numerous industry awards for her famous ad campaign: "We Put the Smiley Face in the D☺t in Dot-Com."

YOUR MILEAGE MAY VARY, BUT . . .

Some experts suggest limiting your management section to as few key players as possible; others recommend including all the top guns in your management arsenal. In general, however, most concur that these positions or functions should be covered:

- Chief executive officer (CEO)
- Chief information officer (CIO), if relevant to the nature of your business
- Chief financial officer (CFO)
- Sales and marketing VP or director

Depending on the size of your organization and its product or service, you may also want to include or at least mention such positions and functions as:

- Lead engineer
- User interface specialist

- Operations specialist
- Key consultants and/or experts

On the last item, suppose you are creating a research resource for college professors; a list of your experts and areas covered or experience would assist in showing your ability and preparation. Also, if you know that you will need to enlist consultants or experts and have not even begun to research just whom you will hire, now is the time. Researching these individuals' qualifications and selecting them will let you evaluate whether their roles in your organization will help you make your business case. If your evaluation is affirmative, you'll definitely want to include information about them in this section.

Should you create an organizational chart and include it here? This question is also an area of debate. However, I would recommend creating it and then including it in your appendix with the résumés of your key players. This will help readers see just how you are deploying the experience of the individuals whose résumés are included.

In addition, don't forget to address any legal issues pertaining to your site. Potential legal elements range from your company's legal structure (e.g., sole proprietorship, general or limited partnership, corporation, limited liability company) to its ability to comply with government and regulatory matters relating to your operations.

RECRUITING

If your initial creation of an organizational chart indicates that you are missing some needed skills—for example, you have no one on your team with any experience in marketing—you may need to undertake some recruiting efforts. Don't dismiss the possibility of a partnership. For example, if you know someone who (1) has the skills you need, and (2) has a small non-Web consulting business, you may want to meet with that individual and explore the possibility of forming a partnership. That would give your partner Internet exposure and fulfill your need— ideally, without requiring any extra expenditures.

However, if you do decide that you need to hire someone to fill a missing function, start with one of the best recruiting methods available: your colleagues. Ask them to pass the word to their friends. Tell your relatives. Notify your dentist. Word of mouth (pardon the dental pun), also known as networking or schmoozing, is one of the best ways to recruit talented employees.

Andrew Beebe, cofounder and CEO of Bigstep.com (see Figure 4-2), notes, "We've hired strength in the senior team, and they in turn have attracted A players. The networks of our own employees are proving more powerful than any recruiters out there." Here's Beebe's advice to those who would follow in his dot-com footsteps: "Stick to your passions, and be honest and frank—first with yourself, then with everyone you work with."

In addition, check with your college's or university's career placement center and alumni services. Both may have a section dedicated to job postings—and, as a graduate, you may be entitled to post your job openings for free. In addition, check with applicable organizations and associations. They also often have job posting sections that are free to employers.

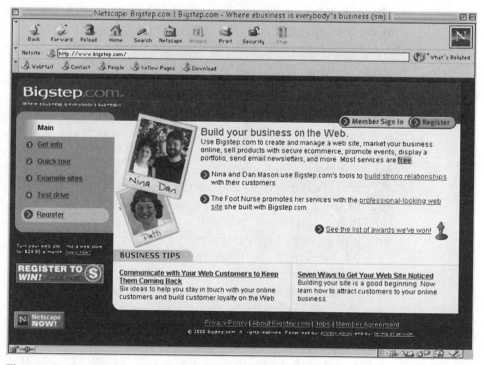

Figure 4-2. Says the founder of the popular Web site Bigstep.com: "Stick to your passions."

If you do want to purchase advertising, here are some of the most popular career sites:

- *CareerMosaic (http://www.careermosaic.com/)*. This site offers information about online job fairs as well as a place to post a job.
- *CareerPath (http://new.careerpath.com/)*. Similarly organized, this site is highly popular with job seekers.
- *MonsterBoard (http://www.monster.com/)*. This site is a standard on lists of recommended job resources online.
- *Yahoo! (http://dir.yahoo.com/business_and_economy/employment/jobs/index.html)*. For a variety of choices, including job directories, good ol' Yahoo! has another winner.

UNCLE SAM HAS ADVICE, TOO

The U.S. Small Business Association's Web site has suggestions on creating the management plan for your business. In addition, the SBA has a good description of the challenges in managing your own business: "Managing a business requires more than just the desire to be your own boss. It demands dedication, persistence, the ability to make decisions and the ability to manage both employees and finances. Your management plan, along with your marketing and financial management plans, sets the foundation for and facilitates the success of your business."

The SBA also emphasizes the role of your managers and staff, noting that your employees "are the most valuable asset a business has. You will soon discover that employees and staff will play an important role in the total operation of your business. Consequently, it's imperative that you know what skills you possess and those you lack, since you will have to hire personnel to supply the skills that you lack."

Make sure that your management section addresses just how your key players qualify in areas in which you do not have sufficient experience. Ask for their input as well. As the SBA says, "It is imperative that you know how to manage and treat your employees. Make them a part of the team. Keep them informed of, and get their feedback regarding, changes. Employees oftentimes have excellent ideas that can lead to new market areas, innovations to existing products or services, or new product lines or services which can improve your overall competitiveness."

Checklist

Based on the SBA's guidelines and recommendations from entrepreneurs and venture capitalists, here are some items to include in the management section of your plan:

☐ Describe clearly and succinctly your own management background and visions and those of each member of your management team. Note that the résumés of the key founders and management are included in the plan's appendix. However, don't make the common mistake of thinking that your readers will immediately leap to the appendix and pore through each and every résumé. It's up to you to summarize that information in a way that convinces potential investors up front that you've got a team worth their money and commitment. Be complete and concise as you list the qualities and experience that your managers possess.

☐ Make it clear precisely how your background and business experience qualifies you for your position and e-business.

☐ If your description of your background and experience reveals weaknesses (e.g., if you have absolutely no background or experience in budgeting and finances), make it clear how you can compensate for those drawbacks. (In line with the former example, you might emphasize the extraordinary skills and experience of your CFO.)

☐ If certain members of your management team have strengths that compensate for others' weaknesses, describe precisely how they complement one another, demonstrating that the overall management team is strong in every area.

☐ Delineate the duties of each member of your management team, making it clear how the organization lines up. Again, although you can refer readers to an organizational chart in the appendix, you need to demonstrate in this section that you've thought through your e-company's organization and have clearly defined the responsibilities and duties of each member, as well as the reporting structure.

☐ Detail your current personnel needs and plans for hiring and training personnel.

☐ Include any legal issues (e.g., proprietorships, partnerships) and, if applicable, consultants and/or board of directors.

5
The Competition

Is it really a jungle out there, packed cheek to jowl with ferocious CEO tigers and ravenous CFO bears? Well, yes and no.

I'll give you an "aye" if you are referring to the fact that no matter how tranquil you may think your chosen e-market is, there's always the possibility of another e-biz chieftain marching in and invading your territory. Or an online giant, like Amazon.com, licking its thirsty lips and humming, "Hmmm, looks mighty tasty," as it stomps without warning into your market.

But I respond with a firm "nay" if you are worrying that it's a mite too crowded out there in Webland.

Consider the advice of Laura Stanford, CEO of Pro-Se-Sports.com: "Go for it, but don't expect anything to happen quickly or easily." Her goal—to "sell branded women's athletic apparel online only," featuring "products that perform well, look good, and are reasonably priced in a wide-reaching channel"—has been achieved. And, as evidenced by her caution about not expecting a quick ride to Easy-Street-Dot-Com, Laura has succeeded by striving to outdo her competition. And that requires locating and analyzing those competitors.

Stanford is just one example of an entrepreneur who dreamed a dream, recognized that she had competition—and did it anyway.

One of the experts in this area is PricewaterhouseCoopers's national director of emerging company services, located in San Jose. After reviewing hundreds of high-tech business plans, Steve Bengston has a unique perspective on the future of e-commerce. I asked him whether he felt that the opportunities are endless, or whether competition on the Internet is getting so intense that only a few can make it. "The Internet will change virtually every industry," predicts Steve, "so this is the start of a 20-year revolution. Only two to three companies in each category will matter and make it, but there will be hundreds of categories."

With that prediction in mind, it's time to focus on the competition in your category. And this includes potential challengers: businesses not currently online but aiming at the same market—and fully capable of moving to the Internet at any time.

SPELL IT OUT—AND SEARCH IT OUT

You will need to specify precisely what you offer that makes you distinct as you discover and analyze each competitor. Your goal: to show just how you are positioned as the dot-com of choice. One way to begin this process is to utilize search engines and directories to locate your competition. See the Dot-Com Directory in Part Two for details and suggestions for search engines.

As an example, if I were seeking out the competition for Grrlbiz.com, I would enter searches utilizing phrases such as "girls + entrepreneurs," "teenagers + finance," and "business + youth." Here are just a few samples of search and directory Web sites and how they work:

- *Search IQ* (*http://www.searchiq.com/*). This elegantly designed Web site offers assistance on how to make your search easier and faster. It also includes a list of the top-ranked search engines and a directory of specialty directories.

- *Yahoo!* (*http://www.yahoo.com*). This grandpapa of the search engines and directories still ranks high on my list. It's well organized, simple, and well designed.

- *AltaVista* (*http://www.altavista.com*). Ask Jeeves has received a lot of hype for its ask-the-question, get-the-answer style. But AltaVista offers the same tool, plus the ability to search by just a few words and/or use categories.

- *Hotbot* (*http://www.hotbot.com/*). Many of my techie friends claim Hotbot as their favorite. What it offers, in addition to categories and a standard search feature, are such up-front advanced tools as searching by date (e.g., the last week, the last year), language, URL, and/or media type.

- *Google* (*http://www.google.com/*). The name may make you smile—and the odds are high that the results will too. The results include not just a URL but also a short section of the text that matches your search query. A major time-saver.

You may also come up with some additional information on your competition when you research your market, as described in the next chapter. One important note in this area, in case you're considering outsourcing or skipping lightly over this task. Steve Bengston of PricewaterhouseCoopers says: "Market research can and should be done by the team itself. Talk to 20 prospects, in person, by phone, or over the Internet; get their reaction. You don't need a finished product to talk to prospects. Referrals to research reports like Forrester and others are not that helpful since the numbers are always huge and the market definitions are too broad. Better to have 40 percent of a smaller market than 4 percent of a larger one."

He also warns that the most common mistake that entrepreneurs make in the development of their business plans is "not talking to prospects to get their validation of the concept." In addition to seeking out search engines for Turnip-Chips.com (where I'd use key words and phrases such as "health foods," "online fitness," "virtual nutrition," and "healthy snack foods"), I would make sure that my competitive analysis team researched health and fitness publications, looking at the ads and product reviews, to see what similar products, if any, were advertising and/or had already achieved PR. I'd also ask my team to visit health clubs, health food stores, and sports stores, interviewing consumers on what products they enjoy for guilt-free snacking.

ADDING DEPTH TO YOUR COMPETITIVE ANALYSIS

Let's start the process by viewing the Small Business Administration's advice. The SBA, courtesy of Uncle Sam (and your tax dollars), offers these comments and recommendations on the competition section of your business plan now and as you develop your plan during the life of your business:

> Competition is a way of life. We compete for jobs, promotions, scholarships to institutes of higher learning, in sports—and in almost every aspect of our lives. Nations compete for the consumer in the global marketplace as do individual business owners. Advances in technology can send the profit margins of a successful business into a tailspin, causing them to plummet overnight or

within a few hours. When considering these and other factors, we can conclude that business is a highly competitive, volatile arena. Because of this volatility and competitiveness, it is important to know your competitors.

Questions like these can help you:

1. Who are your five nearest direct competitors?
2. Who are your indirect competitors?
3. How are their businesses: steady? increasing? decreasing?
4. What have you learned from their operations? from their advertising?
5. What are their strengths and weaknesses?
6. How does their product or service differ from yours?

Start a file on each of your competitors. Keep manila envelopes of their advertising and promotional materials and their pricing strategy techniques. Review these files periodically, determining when and how often they advertise, sponsor promotions, and offer sales. Study the copy used in the advertising and promotional materials, and their sales strategy. For example, is their copy short? descriptive? catchy? or how much do they reduce prices for sales? Using this technique can help you to understand your competitors better and how they operate their businesses.

RECOGNIZE THE NEW CHALLENGES IN THE INTERNET ERA

The challenge posed by the Internet to sellers is the ease with which buyers can analyze their purchasing options. From Priceline.com, where would-be buyers can name their own price, to Compare.com, where browsers can evaluate costs and quality with the click of a button, there are a wide range of sites designed to give consumers the power.

So, how do you compete in this brave new world? Mentally become a customer, a potential purchaser of your product or service. Making yourself think like a consumer, not a seller, is the *only* way to make the most out of your e-commerce opportunity. Depending on your product or service, the analysis that you must go through will vary. But the process is basically the same. You must play the role of both seller and customer by asking and answering these questions.

1. What Added Value Do You Bring to Your Customers or Clients?

For example, do you solve a problem for your potential customer or client? Do you seek to entertain? Do you fill a need that the customer might not even be aware of? Or are you providing a resource? Now imagine that you're a customer who faces that problem, has that desire for entertainment, or is in need of that resource. What would you do? Whom would you consult? Where would you look?

Depending on what your product or service is, your customer or client might consult industry publications, associations, library reference books, the Internet, and/or a government agency. Check out these same sources, wearing your "customer" hat, and you'll discover additional competitors. And keep notes of those sources—because once your site is open for business, you'll want to make sure that you're listed with those same resources!

2. What Do Those Competitors That You Have Discovered Offer?

Garbed in your "customer" attitude again, consider your options for purchasing the service or product. What's offered by each one? And what's lacking?

Let's use Grrlbiz.com as an example. First, I would ask different educational and scholastic groups and related associations for recommendations. For example, I might talk to leaders of the Girl Scouts and Camp Fire Girls, Junior Achievement officials, PTA groups, and so on. I'd check out the relevant publications, post notes to mailing lists and newsgroups, and let my mouse do the walking through the various search engines and directories.

Among the competitors that I'd discover would be the Young Entrepreneur's Association (http://www.yeo.org/) and Startuprx (http://www.startuprx.com/). For each competitor that I discovered, I'd follow the SBA's advice and set up a folder, evaluating each one on details such as what it features, what it lacks, and its quality, service, and so forth.

I would sleuth out additional details by probing relevant mailing lists and newsgroups in depth, as well as reading industry publications and checking on what analysts say about each competitor. You'll find information on how to locate mailing lists and newsgroups, as well as the best industry publications, in the Dot-Com Directory in Part Two of this book.

You must also evaluate your plans for pricing, and the current pricing strategies of your competition. The SBA views your pricing strategy as a method for improving your competitiveness. The agency recommends that you "get a feel for the pricing strategy your competitors are using. That way you can determine if your prices are in line with competitors in your market area and if they are in line with industry averages."

Some of the pricing strategies include:

- Retail cost and pricing
- Competitive position
- Pricing below competition
- Pricing above competition
- Price lining
- Multiple pricing
- Service costs and pricing (for service businesses only)
  - Service components
  - Material costs
  - Labor costs
  - Overhead costs

The key to success is to have a well-planned strategy, to establish your policies, and to constantly monitor prices and operating costs to ensure profits.

SIT IN YOUR POTENTIAL CUSTOMER'S CHAIR

Stay focused on your customer throughout your analysis. This focus will enable you to ask the same questions that your customers will ask as they decide whether to purchase from you or one of your competitors. Here are four main considerations:

- What do you have that your competition lacks?
- What do competitors have that you don't?

- Do you offer more variety but higher prices?
- Do you feature outstanding guarantees, service, and promises of complete satisfaction—but fewer selections?

Clarify just what you have that would lure customers away from the Other-Guys-dot-com to your Web site. What makes you unique?

Red-Flag Warning: You must understand and be able to describe how you will compete against the existing challengers in order to procure funding. A major red flag to potential investors is a statement such as, "Oh, well, I don't have any competition." Wrong. What that statement really says is, "Oh, well, I didn't take the time to see who else is out there." It may be comforting to play ostrich and hide your head when it comes to evaluating the playing field, but it sure won't win you any supporters—or customers.

ACHIEVING "CUSTOMER-MINDED" ATTITUDES

Maintaining your "customer mentality" is critical to helping you achieve your goals. How can you stay customer-minded?

Well, here's another way to look at the attitude that I urge you to develop. Have you ever purchased a complex electronic product, gotten it home, eagerly opened the box—and then stared, baffled, at the assortment of gizmos, gadgets, widgets, and wires tangled together? You hunt for an operating manual. Bolts, bits, and baffling buttons—it's a jungle of a jumble! Finally, at the bottom of the mess, your search is rewarded. A smudged, one-page sheet written in jargon so technical that not even the whiz kid next door can help!

Frustrated, you attempt to call technical support. And "attempt" is the name of the frustrating game. Five tries later, you hear, not a busy signal, but a recording that says, "Due to the popularity of WidgetWhiz's offerings, the estimated wait for customer service is 30 minutes to three hours." Elevator music begins playing as you glare at the telephone receiver. You slam everything back into the box, and return to the store to demand a refund. "I'll never buy from WidgetWhiz again," you vow.

Now, there's an example of an entrepreneur who was the opposite of customer-minded. So remember how you feel in such circumstances—and let your customer mentality keep you out in front of your competition.

VISIT THE ENEMY

Don't hesitate to tread on enemy territory. Visit competitors' Web sites. Go through the shopping process there. Become a customer—and see how the service rates. Take detailed notes, evaluating the products or services, prices, quality, variety, site design—every aspect of what the competition has. Know thy enemies—and learn from them. And remember: you should continue exploring your competition throughout the life of your business. Just as you will want to keep your business plan alive by continually updating it and referring to it as needed, so you must keep your eye on the competition.

Here are some points to review when you visit your competitors' Web sites and read about them in industry publications:

- What do their press releases and corporate biographies reveal about their future plans? Is the company forming partnerships? Is it edging toward new terrain?

- Check to see if competitors quote commendations from industry analysts and publications on their Web sites—and make a mental note to send your press releases and other information to those same sources.

- Look at their job postings. What types of jobs are they advertising for? The answer can reveal their current status and future.

- Are competitors' concepts and even Web site names "too close for comfort" to yours?

Consider one of my "pet" examples of competition: online pet stores. There's the remember-my-name winner, Pets.com, which Amazon.com chose as its partner. Then there's the formerly dubbed PetJungle.com, which became Petsmart.com when "real-world" pet store Petsmart Inc. extended an invitation to partner. Also running doggedly in this race for attracting owners of four-legged friends are

Petopia.com and Petstore.com. Want more choices? No problem. There's also PetExpress.com.

Suppose that I came up with a formula for a liver-flavored version of Turnip Chips that was shown in testing both to be good for and to appeal to dogs? If I decided that I wanted to market those chips by creating a pet section in Turnip-Chips.com, I'd have to consider the multiple strengths of each competitor in the furry-friends realm. Pets.com, for example, has an impressive selection of products, interesting content, and solid customer service. Petsmart.com, however, will win existing customers of the retail Petsmart who want to go shopping online. The others have similar advantages.

Ouch. What I would need to do is figure out what pet owners really want that these sites don't offer—and fill that niche. Or (ideally "and") I'd have to evaluate what they do—and do it better. An alternative would be to decide that I wanted to expand and go B2B (business to business) by selling the Liver Turnip Chips wholesale to existing pet sites and pet stores.

Here's what Tim Knight, one of the key executives at Prophet Financial Systems (see Figure 5-1), has to say about analyzing the competition—and then using that analysis to improve your own chances of success. Prophet (ProphetFinance.com) "provides Internet-based software applications and information that help self-directed investors make more profitable trading decisions."

In order to check out his competition, Tim looked at his past experiences, his competition, and his preferences. "Over the years I've spent a considerable—sometimes excessive—amount of time on my trading. I can honestly say that I've used products from our competitors (as well as our partners) from a trader's perspective. Prophet's products tend to reflect my own biases in terms of what I use and look for," says Tim.

He admits to being "a bit of a data freak, and I'm a fanatic about order. I'm always trying to streamline and arrange things in ways that make sense. Once I decided to learn a technical analysis software program that sells for thousands of dollars. I was sure it was going to make my trading more profitable. I'm a pretty computer-literate guy, but this software just seemed way too complicated. I never got used to it."

Using the "invent a better mousetrap" philosophy, Tim "found the features I liked most and designed ProphetCharts. Now it's all I use."

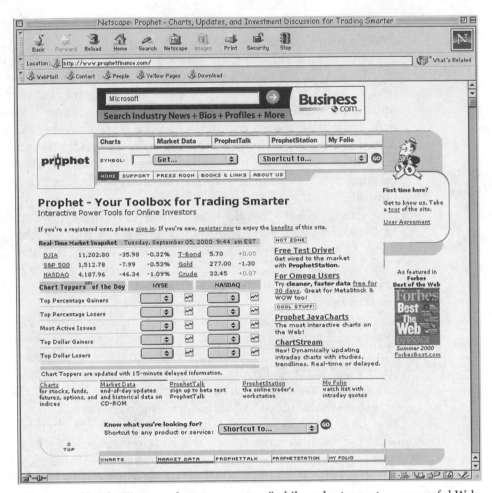

Figure 5-1. Use the "invent a better mousetrap" philosophy to create a successful Web site such as ProphetFinance.com.

WHAT'S UP AHEAD?

In addition to evaluating your current competition, look for possible future competitors. Take the time to read industry publications (you'll find a list and descriptions in the Dot-Com Directory). And continue reading them. You'll get ideas not only about your direct competition but about your business in general. For example, Interactive Week (interactive-week.com) has a regular feature comparing two sites in its Head2Head section.

Remember: it's a dog-eat-dog world, especially if you're competing for pet owners!

Checklist

In summary, you've analyzed your competition realistically *only* if you've taken the time to do the following tasks, the results of which should be summarized in your business plan:

☐ Sleuth out and discover the products and services that compete with your dot-com business. Describe the companies that produce those products and/or provide those services, clarifying how your product or service wins over each competitor.

☐ Evaluate and analyze your competition, both the major players and the minor players. In "Internet time," a just-got-started minor player could become a major player tomorrow. Read all that you can find about each one, from the management team to the type of publicity that the competition has garnered. Make it clear in this section of your business plan that you are not just shrugging off the fact that competition exists: you've analyzed your competitors, and you can show how you will outrun them.

☐ Set up files or databases to track and evaluate each competitor, analyzing and comparing the product and/or service as well as any relevant factors such as performance and results, Web site design and downloading speed, customer service, pricing, advertising, technical support (if applicable), shipping and handling, availability, purchasing mechanisms and security, and guarantees, return policy, or warranties (a major reason that some consumers were upset with Internet sites in the postholiday-purchase-return period). If there are areas in which your site is clearly stronger than any of the competition, list those areas in this section of your plan.

☐ Before you conclude the section, review what you've written. Make sure that you have detailed the pros and cons of every competitor and demonstrated in what ways your dot-com business will beat your competitors.

6

Your Market and Customer

I once had a friend who called me at midnight to share his Bright Idea-dot-com. "You know how I absolutely love foods that gross out a lot of people," he excitedly began.

"Yup," I said, yawning and shuddering at the same time as I recalled his fondness for concoctions such as peanut-butter-and-sweet-pickle-on-raisin-bread sandwiches.

"Well, I'm going to start a Web site and market that stuff," he said. "It'll make a fortune. I'm gonna call it something like 'Say It Loud and Say It Proud, Gross Foods Are Rad!' Whaddya think?"

I said I had some questions: "Who are your prospective customers? What's your target market? And once people sample something like your lime gelatin salad made with crushed potato chips, mayonnaise, and red-dye-number-2 gummy bears, how many will return?"

Silence. Then the phone slammed down. Like I said, I once had a friend . . .

WHO IS YOUR CUSTOMER?

To rephrase my ex-friend's slogan, "Say it loud and say it proud: understanding your customer is essential!" To elaborate on that concept, you need to make it clear in your business plan that you can clearly and correctly describe your customer and target market, *and* that you have a product or service that the customer and market you've pinpointed will purchase.

> **Red-Flag Warning:** Consider it a redder-than-an-embar-
> rassed-beet flag if you cannot identify any prospective cus-
> tomers other than yourself (and maybe your mother, if she is as
> loyal as mine).

As the Small Business Administration says: "The key element of a successful marketing plan is to know your customers—their likes, dislikes, expectations. By identifying these factors, you can develop a marketing strategy that will allow you to arouse and fulfill their needs. Identify your customers by their age, sex, income/educational level, and residence."

As you work on this section, focus, at least initially, on identifying and reaching the customers or clients who are most likely to purchase your product or your service. Be sure you cover the following areas:

- Describe your customers or clients and target market.
- Evaluate your market. What is its growth?
- Describe the ways in which you will attract customers or clients and retain them.

For example, prospective customers at Grrlbiz.com are young girls and teenagers. In this section of the plan, I would point to the rapid increase in adolescents who are using the Internet and their growing sophistication about and interest in finance. I would cite statistics on this increase and note how the discussion boards and opportunities to make money would attract and retain these young women.

One way to learn more about what your prospective customers really want is to create focus groups. One Internet entrepreneur, Frank Levy, utilized this customer research method in creating the concept for PlanetAll.com.: "PlanetAll.com is a contact management service where your address book is maintained by the people in it. We interviewed college and graduate students in Boston while we were developing the concept. The founders were looking for something that captured the universality and community aspects of our service concept. PlanetAll seemed to resonate with our focus groups."

Asked what he would have done differently, knowing what he knows now, Levy adds, "I think we would have probably tried to find a way to provide more instant gratification to the user, and we would have simplified the user interface."

Depending on your product or service, other methods of identifying your customer and tailoring your offering to your customers' needs and interests include questionnaires, test marketing, usability tests, and pilot programs or "soft" or "staggered" rollouts. For example, customer and market research for Turnip-Chips.com could include questionnaires, taste tests, and samples in health clubs, health food stores, and similar outlets, with free samples sent to editors at health and fitness publications and Web sites, inviting them to comment on and review the product.

PLAYING THE NUMBERS

Three words of warning about citing statistics: tell the truth. You are writing for readers who are highly savvy about the Internet market—and "massaging" statistics will bring you nothing but a rejection letter. Check your facts. Then double-check them. And be sure to cite not only your sources but the dates on which the relevant statistics were reported. You don't want a potential investor looking up your source—and discovering that the trend chart around which you built your entire product line was created in 1965.

Elizabeth Slocum, e-consults.com founder, feels that market research is "very, very, very important. As a marketer, I would be a threat to my profession if I didn't stress the importance of research. Everything—the brand strategy, the look and feel, the tagline, advertising, packaging, pricing, and so forth—ties into the target market. And the best way to define and segment the target market is through research. With the advent of the Internet, there is a ton of data to be found and incredible new ways to obtain real-time primary research. Again, everything is easy (easier?) once the target market has been defined."

For more information on market research, including my recommendations for useful Internet resources, see the Dot-Com Directory in Part Two of this book. Once you have your research accomplished, use it.

"Duh, that's obvious," you might be thinking.

Maybe. But a very common mistake is to assume that it is sufficient to dump information such as market projections into this section of your plan. Wrong. As you write the market and customer section, focus on the implications of those statistics for your product or service. For example:

- Do your statistics fully apply to your customers? Suppose that I cite statistics saying that more female adolescents want to become entrepreneurs—as proof that Grrlbiz.com will be successful. That wouldn't be enough. I would also need to show that female adolescents are spending more time online, since my product and service are offered on a Web site. In other words, I need to draw conclusions for my readers (and be truthful about them!).

- Do you have a clear understanding of your customers or clients? Can you describe, for example, their purchasing patterns? Their hobbies? If relevant, their location?

- What do your customers need, want, and enjoy? How does your product or service fulfill at least one of those areas?

- How large a market share will you have? How will you keep it? And how will any subcategories of your offerings affect your main product or service? Suppose that Turnip-Chips.com decides to sell a product that allows consumers to create Turnip Chips in their homes in less than two minutes. If that product proved successful, all efforts by Turnip-Chips.com to publicize, manufacture, and sell its various flavors of Turnip Chips—and all the time and expense that went into the fitness and nutrition area—would be money down the drain. Now what?

The Small Business Administration advises: "At first, target only those customers who are more likely to purchase your product or service. As your customer base expands, you may need to consider modifying the marketing plan to include other customers." In addition, the SBA recommends that you analyze your market by profiling your customer. This involves determining the sector to which you will primarily be selling. Also indicate how you will be targeting customers (e.g., your product line and/or service), your target industry, and statistics on how much your selected market will spend on your type of product or service in subsequent years.

A MEDITATIVE MOMENT, PLEASE

Here are some points that you should consider in creating the market and customer section.

All Customers May Not Be Created Equal . . .

Suppose, for example, that you have targeted three very different markets for three highly distinct product lines: people who are left-handed, self-proclaimed "computer illiterates," and single-parent households. The age range, gender, and level of technical knowledge clearly would differ considerably, and you would need to describe a profile customer for each market in your business plan.

Name That Game

Make sure that you can clearly define the industry in which you are involved, as specifically as possible. For example, since Turnip-Chips.com plans to offer fitness and nutrition information online, it is essential to define just who that audience would be. If I based my entire market analysis and customer profiles on all individuals, cited statistics for all people in general, and developed financial projections on this model, I would significantly overestimate the Turnip Chips market and probably spend more on the initial outlay than was warranted.

What Do Customers Buy—and Want?

Evaluating your customers' buying habits is another key to creating this section of your business plan. And a major "don't" here is: never, never make assumptions. Suppose, for example, that I plan to create a Turnip-Chips.com product line that consists of Turnip Chips that taste like peanut butter and grape jelly. My basis for this decision? A friend's comment that her son will eat anything, from carrots to broccoli, that is topped with peanut butter and grape jelly.

Assuming from this statement that all children like anything that tastes like peanut butter and grape jelly, I spend considerable time and energy producing such a product. But suppose that instead of basing my decision on this single individual, I decide to research her comment.

Suddenly I discover that children like the texture and "mouth feel" of peanut butter and grape jelly just as much, if not more, than the taste.

Find out what your customers purchase, what they want, what they need, and what they think of your proposed product or service by interacting with them as much as possible.

Tip: Numerous resources for finding information on customer preferences are listed in the Dot-Com Directory in Part Two. Here are some of the best:

- U.S. Department of Commerce (http://www.doc.gov/)
- Current Population Survey (http://www.bls.census.gov/cps/cpsmain.htm)
- Marketing Center (http://www.marketingsource.com/)
- Jupiter Communications (http://www.jup.com/)
- Emarketer.com (http://www.emarketer.com/)
- Electronic Commerce Guide (http://ecommerce.internet.com/)
- Patricia Seybold Group's Customer.com (http://www.customers.com/)
- CyberAtlas (http://www.cyberatlas.com/)
- IDC's Internet section (http://www.idc.com/data/internet/)
- American Statistical Association (http://www.stat.ncsu.edu/info/srms/srms.html)
- USGS's Web site on market research (http://www.usgs.gov/customer/page13.html)
- IntelliQuest's research tools (http://www.intelliquest.com/tools/)
- Frost and Sullivan's market engineering newsletters (http://www.frost.com/newsletter/)
- Council of American Survey Research Organizations (http://www.casro.org/)

CUSTOMER CARE

New media research firm Jupiter Communications recently reported that "90 percent of online customers prefer human interaction." And Net Effect Systems (which specializes in customer service) released the results of a study in summer 1999 showing that 67 percent of online purchases are never completed. Virtual shopping carts are abandoned—mainly because of the lack of "real" customer service.

What this means is that unless your target market consists of antisocial hermits, you must plan thoroughly just how your customers want to be treated. So, evaluate every area of customer interaction, from the first visit to your site to the site experience to purchasing to follow-up and return policy. Although I'll discuss this essential in subsequent chapters as well, I regard it as a key element of your market and customer section as well. Neglecting to consider the need to establish your reputation with customers is a definite "don't."

Mutual trust and respect are essential—and difficult to establish. A study by Cheskin Research and Studio Archetype/Sapient showed that customer trust develops through repeated exposure to the purchasing experience—not just a one-time visit to a site. What do your customers really want? In most cases, they're seeking just what you look for when you visit a store or a service organization:

- An area that's attractive and easily accessed (e.g., well-lighted, clean, wide aisles). Translated in Web talk, the site is easily viewed, quickly downloaded, and simple to traverse.

- Products that are easy to locate and nicely displayed. For the Web, this means a well-organized site with regard to links and navigation.

- Quick, courteous customer service and checkout. In Webland, this means that if you don't have "real" customer service, make certain that your online help is thorough and polite, and includes some type of e-mail or 800 number answered by a human being.

- Clearly posted and consistently followed return policies, as well as information about privacy guarantees if personal information is sought during the transaction. These policies should be the same for both "real" and virtual stores.

Want an example? Click on over to Amazon.com. Regardless of your browser, it's easy to view. And the wise Amazon.com Web designers there don't make you play games like "Choose whether you want the frames version" or "Click on this aren't-we-clever spinning globe to enter the site." (Such gimmicks might be tolerable the first time you visit a site, but they become an annoyance for repeated visitors.) What you need and want are what you see on your first view of the site:

- Products organized by subject
- An invitation to browse
- A way to get help
- Instant access to the customer guarantee policy

Delving into the site yields such "perks" as media reviews, book excerpts, and (for that "more than 15 seconds of fame" feeling) the opportunity to publish your own book review. Plus, by registering your name, e-mail address, and preferences, you can even sign up for a newsletter and personalize your Amazon.com experience.

Even better, try buying a book from Amazon. You'll get an e-mail response about the status of your order—and, if you respond to that e-mail, a personal response to your e-mail. Service with a virtual smile. Make it a "must" in your planning.

Checklist

Based on the Small Business Administration's advice and the above information, here are some questions to help you complete the market and customer section of your business plan:

- [ ] Who are your customers? Define your target market(s) and the industry.
- [ ] Are your markets growing, steady, or declining? Cite statistics backing up your statements.
- [ ] Is your market share growing, steady, or declining? Cite statistics backing up your statements.
- [ ] Is your market segmented? If so, define and describe each segment.
- [ ] How will you attract, retain, and increase your market share?
- [ ] What are plans for customer care and customer service?

7

Products and Services

Whether you're selling bubble gum or advice on manicuring toenails, your ability to define and describe precisely what you are offering the world on the Web is critical. Yes, potential investors need to be able to evaluate your product or service. But the description that you devise in your product or service section also will be used by your marketing and sales team, in ads and press releases, on your Web site, and by your customer service staff. In summary, the language you choose has implications for the future of your business. So how do you craft this section?

HAVE A SEAT

First, put yourself in your customer's or client's chair. Imagine that someone is describing a product or service to you. What would make you decide to purchase it? As a customer, you probably would base your yea-or-nay purchase decision on the answers to one or more of these questions:

- Does the product or service benefit you in some way?
- Will it make you happy?
- Will it fulfill a need?
- Does it sound like fun?
- Is it unique?

Answering these questions will help you address the second area of this section: the demand for your product or service. "If you build it, they will come" doesn't hold true for Web site businesses. The most

> **Tip:** Whenever possible, include pointers to the appendix throughout your plan. Whether you are offering products or services, attach graphics, photographs or samples if possible. For example, the appendix for Turnip-Chips.com might include photos of the product, with happy and healthy customers of all ages savoring every bite!

gorgeous Web site in the world won't attract many customers if your product or service is as useless as an overheated coffee cup with no handle.

Which brings me to the subject of research. To quantify the demand, you must define your target customer. Focus groups, surveys, usability tests—all are ways to research whether your profiled customer would really want your product or service. One way to tackle this section is to describe the customer experience, from first encountering your Web site through evaluating or learning about the product or service through ordering, customer service, final delivery, and follow-up. And never underestimate the importance of those individuals who actually are in contact with your clients.

Here's a real-life example: I used to shop at a local grocery that had a superb fruit and vegetable section, one that definitely surpassed its competition. I was willing to drive out of my way and pay higher prices because of the superb quality. However, at every encounter that I had with a checkout clerk, I was treated rudely. For example, when I fumbled for change, one clerk snapped, "Hurry up! You're holding up the line."

Another time, when I asked if I could have my purchases bagged in plastic rather than paper, a different clerk refused, saying, "I'd have to go to another counter to get some more plastics, and it's almost my lunch hour."

Then, just to put the sour icing on the unpalatable cake that constituted my customer encounter, I inevitably arrived home to discover that my ripe tomatoes had been squashed under the apples that the clerk had dumped on top of them in the same bag—or that an entire package of croutons had been smashed into crumbs by having a large cantaloupe tossed upon it. When I called the store to complain, I was told, "We don't have a return policy, lady. Next time, bag it yourself."

Well, I'm not a masochist, thank you. There will be no next time with that store.

In summary: show your customers that you value their business. Keep 'em comin' back by training and then valuing your customer service representatives! And demonstrate your awareness of just how essential customer care is by detailing it in your business plan.

Let's use Turnip-Chips.com as an example for preparing your product or service section. As described in previous chapters, the plan is to create and market an original product that looks and tastes like potato chips but is made from turnips. In addition, plans are in place for a gigantic turnip slicer and equipment that will handle every step of the production and manufacturing process fueled by the power of the sun. In the product section, I would describe these plans and, if applicable, any patents on the invention. Now, looking at all this from the reader's perspective (something that every entrepreneur should attempt to do), I might ask, "Hmmm, suppose people are skeptical about just how good those Turnip Chips will taste?" Ah ha! Two secret weapons:

1. The business plan will include testimonies and statistics in the appendix, showing how taste tests conducted across the nation and Canada proved that 99 percent of tasters preferred Turnip Chips over potato chips.
2. Sample packages of Turnip Chips will be shipped with every business plan.

Red-Flag Warning: It's important to prove, as much as possible, that your product is not just "vaporware," as some refer to software that never makes it past the "nice idea" stage. As proof of its viability, the Turnip-Chips.com business plan would include a description of how the chips had already been created and test-marketed to customers whose profiles matched the target audience, and the appendix would include rave reviews taken from customer survey forms. Then, just to whet potential investors' appetites, there would be sample packages of those ever-so-elegant and tasty Turnip Chips.

DEVELOPING THE PRODUCT

If, as in the case of those Turnip Chips, there are product development factors involved, be sure to specify clearly how you have planned for them. For example, in order to have a steady cash flow and keep its product in demand, Turnip-Chips.com's management needs to think about issues such as different flavors of Turnip Chips (e.g., garlic-flavored, barbecue-flavored, chocolate-flavored), planning for how those new products will be developed, tested, and produced. As an entrepreneur, you want your customers not only to "show you the money" once but to keep coming back, buying what you have to offer again and again.

Here's what Brad Garlinghouse, a general partner with @Ventures, the venture capital arm of CMGI, has to say about product development: "It's essential to move quickly. If you use business models of yesterday (e.g., product development cycles of six or more months), your competition will pass you by. Instead, product development is a fluid exercise. Implement a change on your site, see how your users react to it, and then reach to their usage." As an example of this fluidity, Garlinghouse cites eCircles.com, a new Web site described as "a free private place to share with your circle of friends. Share photos, hold discussions, plan group events, and more." That ability impressed Garlinghouse and @Ventures enough to win eCircles.com's founders the backing of CMGI.

IN VENDORS WE TRUST?

Although questions about outside vendors can be handled in your operations section, these issues also need to be covered in your product or service section. If you plan to rely on vendors, describe their qualifications and delivery record.

STANDING OUT IN THE CROWD—A.K.A. OUTSTANDING

What's different about your product or service? What's unique? If the product is really unique, just how are you protecting your concept? Is it patented? Copyrighted? And to what extent is it protected?

Tip: Regarding the area of outside vendors, think twice—and then reconsider—before you sign up with that Ridiculously-Low-Just-Out-of-The-Starting-Gate-Internet-Service-Provider-Dot-com. You may be tempted to go low to save costs when choosing services and vendors. And probably the notion of helping out another new dot-com entrepreneur appeals to you. But you must ask yourself the same questions that both prospective investors and, in some cases, customers may ask you:

- What's this individual's track record or history? If you are starting a new business, including your résumé and experience in the appendix and your background in an "About" section on your Web site are musts.

- What will the site do with the personal information that you provide? Just as you don't want someone to sell your snail mail and e-mail addresses and other details without permission so, your customers want to be reassured that you have a solid privacy policy in place.

- What is the return policy? Your customers will want to make sure that if they have a problem with your product, they will be treated fairly. And you must do the same to protect your investment in items that you purchase.

- What is the quality of customer service and/or technical support? The best product in the world can fail if the customer service and/or technical support is poor.

The key word here is *unique*. Consider, for example, the proliferation of search engines, online directories, and portals. From the relative newcomer Google to the grandpapa Yahoo!, these help-ya-find-what-ya-need options are growing faster than an e-mail virus. So if you have a service or product that's going to be one among the multitudes, you must demonstrate just how it is different enough to attract new customers—and retain them. And don't neglect the legal niceties. If you have registered a trademark, patented a product, or taken other steps to protect your product or service, be sure to include those details.

MONEY, MONEY EVERYWHERE

If you want your share of the seemingly unlimited dollars available from e-commerce, you must calculate the product costs involved. Although you'll be detailing all the financial aspects thoroughly in a subsequent section, product development and related details impact the bottom line as well. So be sure to factor those in.

Checklist

Here are a series of steps to help you complete your e-biz plan.

Step 1: Describe the product and/or service.

Detail the features of your product and/or service and the consumer benefits.

Step 2: Make sure you have included any factors that may cause prospective investors to hesitate.

Emphasize what makes your offerings unique and stand out in the Internet crowd. If you've chosen a category that is already crowded (e.g., the online pets market, with contenders including Pets.com, PetsMart.com, and Petopia.com), be sure to describe just what makes your product or service a guaranteed category-killer. And if it's something that prospective investors may dismiss as "possibly vaporware," specify the stage of your development. For example, in the case of Turnip Chips, I would emphasize that taste tests have already been conducted— and, of course, sample packages of the product would demonstrate my statements.

Step 3: Review what you have written from the point of view of a prospective customer.

Ask yourself: "Would I purchase the product or service from this description?" Make sure that you have included:

☐ Precisely what you are selling or providing.
☐ What the product or service has to offer.

☐ The short-term as well as long-term benefit to the customer. (For example, Turnip Chips taste good, and can extend the customer's lifespan and improve the customer's health.)

☐ The unique aspects of the product or service.

In summary, demonstrate your awareness of focusing on your product or service from the customer's point of view, making it clear that you have analyzed your customers and fully comprehend what they want and what is needed to satisfy them.

8
Marketing and Sales

To market, to market, to sell some fat pigs,
What if my customers prefer to eat figs?

With apologies to Mother Goose, this twisted rhyme sums up just a few of the challenges in marketing and selling your product.

You must have a high-quality product or service ("fat pigs"), set up a way to bring your product or service to the attention of potential customers ("to market"), and offer what those customers want (if it's figs, not pigs, you'd better rethink your scheme). In addition, your product needs to include features (e.g., quality, price, service) that makes your customer choose it over the competition.

By this point in the development of your business plan, you have gathered together the raw material for the marketing and sales section. You've defined your product or service. You know your customer. And you've analyzed what makes you stand out from your competitor. Now you're ready to market and sell your product or service.

ATTRACTION EQUALS PROMOTION

How can you attract the customer that you profiled in the previous sections? By promoting your business. Depending on your product or service, your methods may include:

- Volunteering to speak at relevant conferences or trade shows.
- Sending columns to newspapers and magazines.

- Joining and participating in mailing lists, discussion groups, and other online forums.
- Starting a mailing list or newsletter.
- Using direct mail.
- Placing ads on Web sites and in print publications.
- Joining relevant associations and/or groups.
- Signing up for Link Exchange or other such opportunities.

You'll find more information about these methods in the Dot-Com Directory. You'll need to estimate the costs involved for each method that you choose above. You may initially need to create a marketing budget that's cut to the bone, with the note that you will be expanding your marketing as your business grows. Last but not least, you'll need to answer the question of how much those methods will cost.

For example, for Grrlbiz.com, I would begin by focusing on all the freebies that are available. Announcing my site to newsgroups, Web sites, magazines, and other media for teenagers, parents, and teachers is one good approach. To avoid travel costs, I would initially talk to PTAs and school administrators locally. If I lived near a major U.S. city, such as Los Angeles or New York, I might be able to generate national publicity by contacting the media about any speaking engagements that result from such meetings. These are just a few of the avenues that I would travel to get the message out. My main goal would be promotion of my business initially in as many low-cost/free environments as I could find. The experience would also help me hone in on strategies that worked for the future.

Just remember, as the Small Business Administration advises: "How you advertise and promote your goods and services may make or break your business. Having a good product or service and not advertising and promoting it is like not having a business at all. Many business owners operate under the mistaken concept that the business will promote itself, and channel money that should be used for advertising and promotions to other areas of the business. Advertising and promotions, however, are the lifeline of a business and should be treated as such."

The SBA suggests that you include both advertising and networking as ways to promote your business, with your promos clearly identifying your product or service, Web site address, and price. "Remember the more care and attention you devote to your marketing program, the more successful your business will be."

HOW MUCH IS THAT DOGGIE IN THE WINDOW, AND HOW CAN I BUY IT?

Now that you've decide how to promote your product or service, you need to determine how much you're going to charge, your selling mechanism, and what you will provide in customer service. Your main emphasis here: what will you do to outdo your competition and satisfy your customer?

Marian Banker is president of Prime Strategies (primestrategies.com), a company that provides coaching, consulting, and training in business and leadership. Here's her advice to a would-be Internet entrepreneur putting together a marketing and sales plan: "The first thing to do in creating a marketing strategy and plan is to identify your target market. If you have several potential markets, you might test each market separately. Find out the habits of your target market. What do they read? Are they TV watchers, Web surfers, and so on?"

If you feel that your work in creating the previous sections of your business plan did not answer these questions, seek additional methods of market research. The Dot-Com Directory in Part Two offers more tips on researching your market.

After you've completed this initial step, says Marian, "select the primary medium as your first place to test the market. Be sure to set up an easy way to track the results of each market test. Use what you learn to refine your marketing and maybe even your product or Web site. Think frugal in everything you do. Don't spend money on advertising until you've tested your market and exhausted all the free promotional opportunities on the Web."

Don't underestimate the importance of your marketing and sales plan. "A total marketing strategy is the most important element and should be developed according to the long-term vision and goals for the business," Marian advises. "Then a detailed plan is created based on the strategy. Decide what action you want the Web site visitor to take. Do you just want to gather leads or do you want the visitor to complete the purchase? For situations that would logically require several communications prior to purchase, don't set the site up as a purchase point."

Marian Banker also offers some insights into what you should *not* do: "Common e-commerce marketing mistakes include making the online buying process too complicated and not having an easy way for prospects to get questions answered. If you want visitors to buy online, provide them with as much information as possible—offer a page of frequently asked questions, full details about the company, who the management is, the full address with clear contact information and an explanation of your customer support and service policy."

Remember: slip on that customer hat, sit down in your customer-attitude chair, and imagine that you are a Web site visitor debating over a purchase. What do you want when you evaluate where to purchase an item or service? "Reassure me you're going to be there when I need you," Marian emphasizes.

Once you have that plan in place, you can create a prototype. It might be as simple as a pen-and-paper outline of the buying experience at your Web site, or you could go all the way and set up a mock site. After you've completed this step, "get outside opinions from trusted individuals as to how well you've accomplished your online mission," says Marian.

RITES OF RESEARCH

A little research is a dangerous thing—and ditto for too much. These are words to remember (or put inside a fortune cookie). To elaborate: it's essential to know your market well enough to describe it and evaluate its future. For example, suppose that it is 2991, and you've got a dyna-mite product for the turn of the century. But what about post-3000? Your marketing and sales strategy would need to show how your market will grow increasingly as the time ticks closer to 3000—and also what you would do post-3000.

In the case of Turnip-Chips.com, suppose that I do some research and learn that people around the world plan to spend more money cel-ebrating 2001 than they did celebrating 2000. Consequently, I decide to create a special "Turnip Chip for the Real Millennium," in honor of 2001. Each chip will be branded with the numbers "2001," and each bag will feature a "Happy New Millennium" logo. Initial interest could be high, if I could generate enough publicity (an issue I would also need to address in the marketing section of the business plan). But if I invested significant funds and resources to create these branded chips and packages and manufactured millions, I'd be mighty miserable (not to mention in the red) if all the bags failed to sell before January 1, 2001.

A fad is a fad is a fad is a . . .

When potential investors read your business plan, they want to be assured that you know your market, and that you have done your research. Quantify your statements whenever possible. For example, suppose that, in my Grrlbiz.com business plan, I cite a study showing that 90 percent more teenagers will be online in two years, and I make a grandiose statement about how I will "attract all these teenagers via my marketing plan." I would need to show not only precisely what methods I plan to use to attract them (i.e., my public relations and advertising plan), but just what I will offer to generate sales. See the Dot.Com Directory sections on marketing, advertising, and market research for useful Web sites and related online resources.

SALES AND SERVICE

You can lead a horse to water, but you can't make it drink. The same goes for Web site visitors. Turnip-Chips.com, for example, will be offering a variety of free services, such as Q&A health and fitness advice from experts. If I decide to focus on these services on my home page and not even promote the Turnip Chips there (which is my only income-producing area), the odds are significantly decreased that a prospective customer will happen to come across this little online shop.

Let's be generous, though, and imagine that Turnip Chips are so irresistible that Jo Customer, who read an article about them in her favorite health and fitness magazine, hunts through the site until she finally locates the online shop, which is found under the vague title "Food Boutique."

Jo Customer clicks the boutique link. What greets her are 24 pages of elaborate "How to Purchase" instructions and forms. There's no security guarantee, no customer service phone number or e-mail address, no promises of refunds in case of a problem, and zilch in the way of information about how long it will take her order to be shipped. Bravely, Jo Customer fills out a couple of fields—and then the Web site crashes.

Bye, bye, Jo.

Plan your sales strategy carefully, from the site visitor's first encounter with your product (which should be on the home page) to follow-up. You should address issues such as pricing (as noted in the competition section), quality, and service. For example, you should be clear as to whether you are pricing your services or products above, below, or on a par with your competition. Be sure to account for any materials, labor, and/or overhead involved when you are analyzing your profit. In addition, it can be helpful to look at the different categories of customers. For example, if you are selling to wholesalers as well as retailers, and/or to the government as well as the public, your sales method and strategy may differ for each category.

STRATEGIC THINKING FOR THOSE BABY BOOMER BOXER SHORTS

Be sure to comment on the relationship between your advertising plan and your sales strategy. Suppose that from my extensive research for Turnip-Chips.com, I know that men between the ages of 40 and 60 spend the majority of their online time at sports, automotive, and electronics sites. If I am targeting that age range of men to purchase Turnip Chips, advertising on those portals would make sense. Correlating that plan with my sales strategy, I could base my pricing and customer service plans on profiles of those individuals. For example, additional research might show that they value high quality and fast service much more than whether a product or service is low-priced.

> **Red-Flag Warning:** Before you start gleefully toting up your profit, remember to add in your projected expenses for everything from advertising to phone bills to payroll. And be cautious about quoting market research studies showing a dramatic growth in your market segment. It's a red flag to prospective investors if you fail to include your estimated share of that market and instead plot your sales goals and prices on the naive theory that you will grab the entire market. No company, not even Amazon.com, can make that claim.

SPEC OUT THOSE SPECIFICS

Include details in your plan for online transactions and shipping. Although you will discuss matters such as labor, materials, and suppliers in your operations section as well, you should address those subjects here as well: they will also affect your sales profit and consequently your pricing. And if you haven't started evaluating where you will obtain your materials, supplies, and other items as needed, now's the time to start.

THERE'S A METHOD TO THE MADNESS

Depending on your product or service and your market, you may also need to consider using a variety of sales and service methods. For example, suppose that you are hoping to sell to both children and teenagers. Although some teens do have their own credit cards, very few ten-year-olds do. You'll need to look at alternative purchasing methods, as well as the publicity involved with selling to children on the Internet. Check out ICanbuy.com for an interesting approach to this situation.

Once again, you need to plan every aspect of the customer's experience, from initially learning about your site through advertising to visiting your site and learning about your product or service to purchasing. Include your plans and costs for distribution: shipping methods, packaging, and so forth. And don't neglect customer service. What if the customer has questions during the prepurchase or purchasing process? Suppose the customer is dissatisfied? What is your return policy?

CNETNews.com recently cited a BizRate.com industry study in which "online shoppers rated customer support among the weak links of e-commerce sites" along with a Jupiter Communications report showing that the number of customers who were "largely satisfied" with their online shopping experience had fallen. A Jupiter analyst, according to CNET, "attributed the drop to site failures during the 1998 holiday season," as well as "increased consumer expectations" and the fact that "customers are now holding retailers to the same standards as their offline competitors."

So take the time to plan precisely how your customers will be treated through every phase of their experience with your business.

Checklist

Below are some useful issues to consider, in line with the U.S. Small Business Administration's criteria. (Visit www.sba.gov for additional materials.) Although some of these questions should have been asked and answered in the competition section, this checklist will help ensure that you've covered all essential points.

Market Analysis

A. Target Market: Who Are the Customers?

- 1. We will be selling primarily to (give total percentage of business for each):

    a. Private sector _____%

    b. Wholesalers _____%

    c. Retailers _____%

    d. Government _____%

    e. Other _____%

- 2. How will we be targeting customers?

    a. By product line/services? We will target these specific lines _____

    b. By geographic area? Our primary areas will be _____

    c. By sales? We will target sales of _____

    d. By industry? Our target industry is _____

    e. Other? Describe _____

- 3. How much will our selected market spend on our type of product or service this coming year? $_____

B. Competition

- 1. Who are our competitors?

    NAME _____

    ADDRESS _____

    _____

Years in business _____

Market share _____

Price/strategy _____

Product/service features _____

NAME _____

ADDRESS _____

_____

Years in business _____

Market share _____

Price/strategy _____

Product/service features _____

- 2. How competitive is the market?

  High _____

  Medium _____

  Low _____

- 3. The following are our strengths and weaknesses (location, size of resources, reputation, services, personnel, etc.) compared with those of the competition:

Strengths	Weaknesses
1. _____	1. _____
2. _____	2. _____
3. _____	3. _____
4. _____	4. _____

C. Environment

- 1. The following are some important economic factors that will affect our product or service (trade area growth, industry health, economic trends, taxes, rising energy prices, etc.):

  _____

  _____

  _____

- 2. The following are some important legal factors that will affect our market:

  _____

  _____

  _____

- 3. The following are some important government factors that will affect our market:

  _____

  _____

  _____

- 4. The following are other environmental factors that will affect our market, but over which we have no control:

  _____

  _____

  _____

Product/Service Analysis

A. Description

- 1. What is our product/service and what does it do?

  _____

  _____

  _____

B. Comparison

- 1. What advantages does our product/service have over those of the competition (unique features, patents, expertise, special training, etc.)?

  _____

  _____

  _____

  _____

• 2. What disadvantages does our product/service have?

_____

_____

_____

C. Some Considerations

• 1. Where will we get our materials and supplies?

_____

• 2. What other factors will we consider?

_____

_____

Marketing Strategies

A. Image

• 1. What kind of image do we want to have (cheap vs. good, exclusiveness, customer-oriented vs. highest quality, convenience, speed, etc.)?

_____

B. Features

• 1. Here are the features we will emphasize:

_____

_____

_____

C. Pricing

• 1. We will be using the following pricing strategy:

a. Markup on cost _____ What % markup? _____

b. Suggested price _____

c. Competitive _____

d. Below competition _____

e. Premium price _____

f. Other _____

- 2. Are our prices in line with our image?
      YES___ NO___
- 3. Do our prices cover costs and leave a margin of profit?
      YES___ NO___

D. Customer Services

- 1. Here are the customer services we will provide:

      _____

      _____

      _____

- 2. These are our sales/credit terms:

      _____

      _____

      _____

- 3. The competition offers the following services:

      _____

      _____

      _____

E. Advertising/Promotion

- 1. These are the things we wish to say about our business:

      _____

      _____

      _____

- 2. We will use the following advertising/promotion sources:
      1. Television _____
      2. Radio _____
      3. Direct mail _____
      4. Personal contacts _____
      5. Trade associations _____
      6. Newspaper _____

7. Magazines _____
8. Yellow Pages _____
9. Billboard _____
10. Other _____

- 3. Here are the reasons we consider the media we have chosen to be the most effective:

_____

_____

_____

9
Operations

I'm tempted to head this chapter: OPerations. Why? Because productivity should be your focus here. From selecting your Internet service provider (ISP) to buying a printer to customer service to staffing—any and all of these elements relevant to business productivity should be addressed in the operations section.

This section is sometimes grouped with the management portion of a business plan, and given a label such as Plan of Action. Depending on how thoroughly you documented your management section, however, you may not need to include extensive details about topics such as hiring employees.

In addition, this section's contents will depend largely on the type of business you are starting. For example, in the case of Turnip-Chips.com, I would be setting up an entire manufacturing, production, and shipping operation to create and sell the world's greatest Turnip Chips. Consequently, I would need to cover items such as raw materials and machinery, production issues, and shipping methods. In contrast, my operations or action plan for Grrlbiz.com would focus on what I would need to do to provide business services to young women.

Traci Van Der Vorste-Kaufman is a registered dietitian who created Dietsite.com, one of the most popular diet and nutrition sites on the Internet. She knew that she wanted to provide customers with a place where they could analyze their diets and recipes, as well as get information about diet, nutrition, and fitness. Much of the success of Dietsite.com is due to her attention to the site's operation as well as content.

"Unlike most sites, visits to Dietsite average over 11 minutes and consist of many page views per visit. Sponsors who do sell products and services generate most of our revenue. We do not currently sell products online," said Traci in explaining how her e-biz functions.

"Dietsite was designed as an educational tool for people to learn more about themselves and nutrition." The service is free, and easy to use.

Traci points out that in contrast to retail success, which "relies on such factors as location, inventory management, and access to capital," an Internet business can be successful with only "a computer, ambition, and Microsoft FrontPage. This ease of entry in going online is what keeps all Web business innovating and improving. If you don't keep up, you will be out of business in a nanosecond."

Continual change and growth require planning and the ability to adapt. For Dietsite.com, part of the challenges stems from the fact that it is health-related. Thus, says Traci, "we need to continue our focus on providing the best educational information for our consumers. Like all businesses, we need to turn a profit. However, we cannot put profit ahead of educational focus. This is the biggest challenge for all content-related sites and one we take seriously."

When a potential investor evaluates your Internet business plan, he or she will want to make sure that you are aware of all the challenges awaiting you in Webland. Despite all the media reports of the riches available from venture capitalists, only a select few of would-be Internet entrepreneurs receive financing from the big venture capitalists. Kevin Fong, a general partner at Mayfield Fund offers his perspective on your chances of getting funding with the Mayfield Fund: "We receive about 4000 requests for funding annually, and make between 20 and 30 investments per year," Kevin notes.

"The Internet world is a land grab—it's for the aggressive and bold, not for the meek and timid. Any sales and marketing plan has to focus on capturing the high ground at all cost—it's a winner-takes-all environment that takes lots of money to create the right infrastructure and deliver the right user experience. I'd also focus on building partnerships—the Internet is all about buy, not build. Whom you choose for strategic partnerships says a lot about who you are and creates your brand image and your positioning."

But you can win in the areas of sales and marketing and management—and still bomb out when it comes to operations. Consider, for example, the increased media coverage in regard to two aspects of dot-com business operations: server stability (remember all the press flurry when eBay suffered repeated outages?) and customer service. (A variety of market research reports and surveys showed that customers often left their virtual shopping carts half-filled, and abandoned the online ordering process, because they could not contact a "real"—as opposed to computer—service representative.)

"We're still in the early stages of the Internet," comments Kevin on those areas, "and with any hot new industry, there's a wild and woolly stage where people are forgiving of technical glitches. But I think we are at an inflection point where more and more people are coming on the Internet and starting to rely on it in their lives, so we are getting to the end of the phase when people will forgive companies whose servers can't handle the volume of their business. Companies have to be able to scale seamlessly to meet the increasing demand without damaging the user experience or having lots of downtime."

"We like investing in companies that help alleviate those problems," Kevin continues. "We see that as a natural part of the maturation of the industry. One such investment is Invive, which helps Web sites measure and optimize the performance of their servers. On customer service: at the end of the day, it always matters. Again, it depends where you are on the maturity curve—the earlier you are, the more forgiving your customers. But in the end, if you don't pay attention to customer service, you will fall by the wayside. One of the areas we've invested in is CRMs (customer relationship management companies) which help companies optimize their customer service experience."

As Kevin's comments illustrate, focusing on the quality of the customer's experience when he or she visits your Web site is crucial. The operations section of your business plan must make your plans for and understanding of site management clear.

For example, suppose you want to purchase a book online. You do a general search using Google.com, and discover three different sites that sell the book. The first site that you visit is so slow to download that you give up after a few seconds. When you try to locate the book through the Search field of the second bookseller's site, an error message is displayed instead of search results. But the third try's the charm: This online bookstore's site downloads quickly and has a rapid and efficient search engine and a clearly posted guarantee and return policy.

Now, which site will you visit again? The answer is clear—and you want to make your site the number one choice for your customers as well.

LET'S BEGIN THE OPERATION

As you work on this section of your business plan, you may want to reflect on what you learned from your competitive analysis. How do your competitors' Web sites operate? Can you discover more about their operations and, if applicable, production by revisiting their sites with that focus? Make a purchase, check out their job opportunities area for any leads, and play detective.

Depending on your business, as noted above, you may also need to prepare a manufacturing and production plan. For example, suppose that, to assist in publicizing Turnip-Chips.com, I plan to sell various styles of Turnip-Chips.com T-shirts. In my operations section, I would need to include:

- Information about the design of the T-shirts. Will there be a separate department that produces T-shirt designs? Or will I use a consultant or retail store specializing in that niche?

- Details about the T-shirt production. Will I purchase plain T-shirts wholesale and then take them to an outside source to have the designs applied? Or will I have a department in house to handle that function?

- Packaging, shipping, and handling. Will I purchase boxes or padded envelopes? Will the packaging be done in house? Will Turnip-Chips.com pay for shipping and handling, or will the customer pay for it? Will I offer different types of shipping (e.g., FedEx, priority mail)?

Failing to include these elements and address such issues can become a liability later, when you attempt to evaluate your operating, manufacturing, and/or production costs.

It is important to begin tracking financial components such as costs for materials, labor, and overhead. These figures will be needed to create your financial plan, and you'll want to continue monitoring them. The Small Business Administration advises, "The key to success is to have a well-planned strategy, to establish your policies, and to constantly monitor prices and operating costs."

UNCLE SAM HAS SOME SUGGESTIONS

The SBA regards analyzing your start-up requirements, as well as your ongoing needs, as "the first step to building a sound financial plan."

Tip: If you have devised unique ways of reducing costs and cutting down on overhead, highlight those methods. Demonstrating that you are aware of the need to be cost-efficient can assist you in convincing prospective investors that you're a good risk.

Thus, in your operations section, you can work toward this goal by noting typical costs such as equipment, utility deposits, down payments, supplies, insurance, and rent.

Marian Banker, president of Prime Strategies (which specializes in coaching, consulting, and training in business leadership), warns of some common mistakes in this area: "I've seen capital being put into nonliquid assets (equipment, space, etc.) resulting in too little available working capital. A Web business—like any other—will probably take a year or more to find its way. Decide on the percent profit you want and build that into your goals. Know your monthly expenses and set your sales and collections goals to comfortably cover them. Otherwise, your negative cash flow could eventually pull you under." In other words, investing in the equipment and labor needed to create a complete clothing manufacturing operation for Turnip-Chips.com T-shirts probably wouldn't be a wise business move.

Marian also has some recommendations on how a Web site operates with regard to online purchases, if applicable. You will need to include this information in your operations plan as well. "Decide what action you want the Web site visitor to take. Do you just want to gather leads or do you want the visitor to complete the purchase? For situations that would logically require several communications prior to purchase, don't set the site up as a purchase point," she notes.

Don't forget to keep track of the estimated expenses for any customer service elements. Just like office rentals and services, those costs will need to be calculated into your income projections.

GO WITH THE FLOW

Although you do not need to detail every element of your work and site flow in this section, you do need to plan these areas of your operation.

For example, suppose that you have rented a two-story office building for your business. Your plans call for establishing a research department, a production department, a shipping department, and so forth. How will these groups be situated to make their activity more efficient and productive?

On the "virtual" side of your business, you will need to visualize the flow of your Web site's visitors. Whether you choose to outsource the Web site design or manage it in house, it is critical to consider issues such as the elements you want to appear on your home page, whether you will have links to outside resources, and the purchasing path that users will travel from their first encounter with your home page.

DAY BY DAY

One way to write the operations section of your plan is to envision how your e-biz will function on a day-to-day basis. What will factor into keeping your Internet business open and successful? Focusing on the answer to that question may lead to summarizing your plans and/or purchases regarding:

- Legal regulations
- Rental or leasing issues (for your office or operation and for equipment, if applicable)
- Insurance (both for your employees and for your business)
- Equipment and supplies
- Furniture
- Production process
- Delivery of products and/or services
- Sales expenses, if any (e.g., travel, training)
- Utilities
- Cost of materials, if any
- Storage of inventory, if applicable
- Recruiting, hiring, and salaries of both employees and consultants, as well as executives (plan to give yourself at least a living wage!)
- Telephone bills

- Internet service provider

- Computer hardware

- Computer software

- Additional Web-related expenses (e.g., an electronic newsletter, security, outside IT services, network maintenance)

- Product development, if ongoing (e.g., quality control, performance and reliability tests, usability testing, design work)

- Selection of vendors, if applicable

- Customer service and/or technical support

- Packaging, ordering and payment methods, shipping, return policy, product guarantees, and/or exchange policy

These details will assist in your financial projections. Once again, be sure to note any savings that you are realizing. For example, if I am using an outside accounting firm for Grrlbiz.com and will need the firm's services for only a limited number of hours each month, I could emphasize the cost-effectiveness of this decision initially (as opposed to staffing up a full accounting department).

POLICIES AND PROCEDURES (YAWN)

Before you doze off just thinking about how deadly dull policies and procedures are, please contemplate another "p" word: personalization. If you have registered at Yahoo!, for example, you've experienced this trendy Web marketing tool. Just go to http://my.yahoo.com/ and you'll get welcomed with your user name.

Some companies emphasize the personal touch in their customer service departments. Recently, for example, I initiated a correspondence with Amazon.com's customer service, because I had sent back some items and wanted to know the status of my returns. I received a cheerful, polite response immediately:

Dear Joanne,

Thanks for writing to us at Amazon.com! According to our records, we have not yet received your return. It usually takes between 1 and 2 weeks for the items to be received and processed by our warehouse. When it arrives, our returns department will request the appropriate refund to your credit card. Please don't hesitate to contact us should you have any further questions, and thanks for shopping at Amazon.com! Hello from Amazon.com! Best regards, . . .

You can and should plan for this type of personal touch. And although you shouldn't go into laborious detail, you can include this type of information in your business plan. In your policies and procedures section, you may want to cover how your business will operate with regard to:

- Accounting
- Sales
- Marketing
- Human resources
- Production
- Customer service
- General operations (e.g., shipping and handling, product or service guarantees, online ordering methods, return policies)
- Technical support
- Information systems
- Facilities
- Business development
- Advertising and public relations
- Business hours (for customer service, tech support, employees, etc.)

Concise overviews will suffice, and you probably will not need to include every item listed above. But if an area is critical to your operating success, then you should provide enough information to demonstrate that you have planned for that element. For example, even though your Internet site will be up and running every day of the year, every hour of the day (you hope), it is important to designate specific hours for customer service, tech support, and so on. And, of course, when you're up and running, you will want to return to this section and use it as a basis to create more detailed policies.

> **Tip:** Do not neglect security. Whether you're running a one-person e-biz from your living room or an Internet company staffed with 50 people in a two-story building, attention to both physical and virtual security is critical. From computer backups to passwords to firewalls to office security to controlling site access to—well, you get the picture. For more information on Internet security, visit http://dir.yahoo.com/Computers_and_Internet/Security_and_Encryption/.

DOTTING THE DOT-COM: DETAILED DATA

Last but not least, review the operations section to make sure that you've included and/or accounted for all the Internet-related elements relevant to your business. Think that it's self-evident and runs itself? Rethink that notion. Consider, for example, the statistics cited in a June 2000 article in *Upside* magazine. In 1999, 40 percent of Internet shoppers in the United States experienced online store problems, ranging from shortages of stock to delivery issues to problems even connecting to a Web site. And what did Internet shoppers do when they encountered operational problems at a site? Approximately one-third of them quit that online store and went to another e-biz.

To avoid losing customers, make sure that you've thoroughly researched your selection of every relevant factor, such as:

- Internet service provider
- In-house Web server
- Web master and/or Web designer (or outside Web design firm)
- Computer systems
- Site security

Checklist

Use this checklist to make sure that you've considered all the aspects that may, depending on your e-biz, need to go into the operations section:

> **Tip:** If you haven't yet selected an Internet service provider, now's the time. For assistance, I recommend http://thelist.internet.com/. This site lets you search for an ISP that meets your criteria, and it has an extensive list of providers.

- ☐ Manufacturing, production, storage, and/or shipping
- ☐ Rental or leasing issues (for your office or operation and for equipment, if applicable)
- ☐ Insurance (both for your employees and for your business)
- ☐ Equipment and supplies
- ☐ Furniture
- ☐ Production process
- ☐ Delivery of products and/or services
- ☐ Sales expenses, if any (e.g., travel, training)
- ☐ Utilities
- ☐ Cost of materials, if any
- ☐ Storage of inventory, if applicable
- ☐ Salaries, recruiting, hiring
- ☐ Telephone bills
- ☐ Internet service provider
- ☐ Computer hardware
- ☐ Computer software
- ☐ Product development, if ongoing
- ☐ Selection of vendors
- ☐ Customer service and/or technical support
- ☐ Policies and procedures (i.e., how your business will operate with regard to different departments)

- ☐ General operations (e.g., shipping and handling, product or service guarantees, online ordering methods, return policies)
- ☐ Security
- ☐ Web site services/service provider and any additional Web-related expenses

10

Financial Projections and Financial Management Plan: Going for the Gold (and Green)

Dogged determination and grandiose goals are excellent—but they won't build even a virtual hill of beans without some money. In this section of your business plan, you'll ask potential investors to "show me the money" by demonstrating just how they'll get a return on that money.

Red-Flag Warning: Don't overstate the amount of profit from your business or gloss over obvious risks. You will need to include financial documentation and, if there are clear risks involved, prove that you are aware of and have planned for those risks.

Kevin Fong, general partner of the Mayfield Fund, says that the most common mistakes in this arena are "unrealistic hiring and unrealistic revenue expectations. On the revenue side, we don't see companies having a hard time attracting business. The problem actually is in execution—how quickly can you line up a team and get them executing? There is fierce competition for talent—you've got to have built-in buzz." As a result, Fong warns those who might blithely skip over recruiting concerns, "in some areas that we might like to invest, we aren't, because they will have such a hard time attracting talent in the current environment." For recruiting tips, see the Dot-Com Directory.

This chapter will serve as more than a basis for proving your e-biz's viability to investors. Planning just how your business will become and remain profitable is critical to its success.

William F. McCready of Venture Planning Associates, Inc. notes that when reviewing a business plan, "I personally look for positive cash flow, then profitability, then growth, as the ideal business model. Today's Internet companies think of positive cash flow as the next round of financing. All the acquisition is done with inflated stock and funny money. Doesn't make a lot of sense unless you can return capital and profit at some point, or the well will dry up. We are in an Internet Bubble Economy right now that must come down." McCready adds that the most common mistake made by would-be Internet entrepreneurs is "being focused on their product and technology as opposed to marketing, finance, operations, and product. Just because you can do it better is not a formula for success."

The U.S. Small Business Administration urges new business owners to "plan a sound, realistic budget by determining the actual amount of money needed to open your business (start-up costs) and the amount needed to keep it open (operating costs)."

KNOW THY NUMBERS TOLERANCE

There are those who adore flipping financials, spinning spreadsheets, and coaxing nuances from numbers. Frank Levy of contact management service PlanetAll.com notes that "Warren Adams, the lead founder of PlanetAll, was a classmate of mine at the Harvard Business School, class of 1995. As former consultants and business school grads, we found writing the business plan second nature. The main thing was learning how to tailor it to focus on the venture capital hot buttons of the time: management team and revenue stream."

If you're on the same planet as Frank Levy, the finance section will present no mathematical puzzles. But consider the entrepreneur who, when asked about the finance section, groaned and said, "Don't include my name with this quote. But I am allergic to math. I almost flunked geometry and barely scraped by in algebra. Luckily, my brother-in-law is a CPA and a very nice guy. I bribed him with stock options to write the financial plan for me."

I consider Mr. I-Get-Hives-When-I-Look-at-a-Spreadsheet to be a very wise fellow. He knows his limitations—and he's compensated for them. If that's you, then seek help.

There are many financial experts available. Ask other entrepreneurs for recommendations, and be sure to interview the financial consultants whom you are considering carefully. Review their qualifications and ask for references (and don't neglect to follow up by calling those references and interviewing them as well). If you do choose to go with a financial adviser, you still should take the time to review every element carefully. Ask for help in understanding what you don't understand, from your cash flow and income statements to your balance sheet. A qualified accountant should be willing to explain these subjects and how he or she derived the financial statements.

ELEMENTARY, MY DEAR WATSON

The Small Business Administration recommends that you include these elements in your financial management section:

- Loan applications
- Capital equipment and supply list
- Balance sheet
- Breakeven analysis
- Pro-forma income projections (profit and loss statements)
  - Three-year summary
  - Detail by month, first year
  - Detail by quarters, second, and third years
  - Assumptions upon which projections were based
- Pro-forma cash flow, using the same guidelines as for your pro-forma income projections

If you have already received some funding, be sure to include those figures in your business plan. Create a two-part section: Current Funding and Funding Needed. First list the amounts invested thus far, including capital that you have invested. Then list the additional amount required for your business, such as your start-up requirements.

Your investors also will want to know what you're going to do with those funds. Create another two-part section: Current Use of Funds and Proposed Use of Funds. For example, I have purchased one computer for Grrlbiz.com at $1,019.99. I need two more computers for Grrlbiz.com at that price.

THE WORLD IS MY VILLAGE

If you plan to market and sell in other countries, as is common in our Internet global village world, be sure to allow for shipping currency considerations. For example, you may want to evaluate such items as:

- *Currency exchanges.* Is one of your targeted sectors in a country with major fluctuations in the exchange rate? If so, be careful in how you estimate your profits in that country. To understand what's involved in currency exchanges, visit the Full Universal Currency Converter Web site: http://www.xe.net/ucc/full.shtml.

- *Shipping.* If you feature "free next-day delivery" *and* plan to sell widely outside of the United States, you may want to limit your freebie by adding a qualifier: "within the continental United States." International marketing and selling can be tempting in terms of the potential for expanding your profits—but you need to remember that it's not a straight upward return. Visit your friendly United States Postal Service's Web site for details on international shipping costs: http://www.uspsglobal.com/info/fr_fag.htm. Other helpful sites may be UPS (www.ups.com) and DHL Worldwide Express (www.dhl.com).

- *Taxes.* Even if you aren't marketing and selling outside the United States, you will need to be aware of current Internet taxation laws. The Advisory Committee on Electronic Commerce (http://www.ecommercecommission.org/) was created by Congress and is evaluating all federal, state, local, and international Internet-related taxation and tariffs. Ignorance definitely will not be bliss if you fail to track this and related taxing issues.

Getting assistance from an accountant may be a wise move, depending on your financial prowess. Seek recommendations from other dot-com small business owners and/or check with the certified public accountant association in your state. To locate that organization, visit the American Institute of Certified Public Accountants at http://www.aicpa.org/. Click States, and then click Text Only (it's easier to locate your state than to choose the Map option). For Grrlbiz.com, for example, I would click California, and then scroll down to the State CPA Association.

For many individuals, putting together the financial section of a business plan is the most difficult. And opinions on just what should go in—and shouldn't go in—vary widely.

CONSULT THE INTERNET GURUS

Fortunately, there are many excellent resources on the Internet, which range from sample business plans to interactive put-it-together business plan tutorials to "real world" resources whom you can contact for further assistance.

Here are some of the best:

- The Association of Small Business Development Centers (http://www.asbdc-us.org/) offers a variety of Internet resources. Included are links to the SBDCs in different states. Each SBDC varies in what it provides, and many offer workshops, materials, and counseling. For example, the SBDC located at San Joaquin Delta College (http://www.inreach.com/sbdc/) offers workshops and specific assistance for existing businesses, just-starting-out businesses, women entrepreneurs, and small businesses. The Web site includes extensive information that can be helpful in the finance section of your business plan (http://www.inreach.com/sbdc/book/financial.html and http://www.inreach.com/sbdc/book/financing.html).

- The Service Corps of Retired Executives (http://www.score.org/), also known as SCORE, is another champion of new entrepreneurs. It also often has workshops, counseling, and related assistance. The Web site includes useful links and even free e-mail counseling.

- The Small Business Knowledge Base (http://www.bizmove.com/) has numerous links, including an area devoted to financial management (http://www.bizmove.com/financial.htm).

- American Express has free information about business planning, including an interactive calculator (http://www6.american-express.com/smallbusiness/resources/tools/).

- The Business Owner's Toolkit Web site (http://www.toolkit.cch.com/text/P02_5601.asp) has extensive information on financial management and related topics (http://www.toolkit.cch.com/).

- The Women's Wire's Small Business Web pages (http://www.womenswire.com/smallbiz/mat/) includes a variety of information, including a "toolkit" of topics such as how to estimate startup costs.

- Idea Café (www.ideacafe.com/getmoney/FINANCING.shtml) has brewed a meaty casserole of financing information.

- The SBA (http://www.sba.gov) also has a variety of information on financing with additional tips, as well as useful links.

- So you're saying, "Show me the money, honey!"? Well, at Moneyhunter (www.moneyhunter.com), that's the name of the TV (in this case PBS) show. This Web site is a spin-off of the show, with everything from biz plan templates to a "Golden Rolodex." You will need to register and provide some information about yourself in exchange for the info.

See the Dot-Com Directory for additional financing links.

Lisa Heberley, director of client services at The Interactive Resource, has prior experience with Ernst & Young, Bell Atlantic, and American Express. She earned her BS in accounting at St. Joseph's University in Pennsylvania and her MBA at New York University's Stern School of Business. Here's her advice to an entrepreneur who is hesitant to tackle the financial aspect of his or her dot-com business.

"Rather than officially 'hire' a financial consultant or adviser, an entrepreneur should first seek out advice from associates, colleagues, 'friends of friends,' and anyone else who has experience with starting a business, and then seek additional referrals from these trusted individuals," says Lisa. "MBA students and business professors are other good sources. The more the better, so as to find those advisers whose personalities mesh with the entrepreneur and to expand the knowledge base. These are the people who can offer the honest, blunt, practical advice based upon their experiences. A financial consultant may not be as useful as people who have just gone through this themselves."

WHAT REALLY COUNTS FOR FINANCIAL FIGURES

Here are Lisa's recommendations for putting together your dot-com financial section: "Some of the more important financial elements of an Internet start-up business plan include cash flow projections (cash flow is far more important than profitability for a start-up), sales forecasts, pro forma income projections, a three- to five-year summary, *and* assumptions upon which projections are based. Financial projections for a start-up are based upon assumption on top of assumption on top of assumption."

Is that necessarily a problem?

No, says Lisa, with a caveat. Assumptions are acceptable, if those assumptions "are well documented and supported by solid information. For an Internet start-up, as for almost any business, personnel/management is the key to success and as such, is the most important item for which to budget. Marketing, advertising, and PR are also especially vital."

Her advice to Internet entrepreneurs: "Don't be afraid to seek out an investor in exchange for an equity stake in the company, if necessary, and if the opportunity presents itself. If you're running out of cash fast, sharing your business is better than having no business at all."

Still wondering just how important juggling all those numbers is? The Small Business Administration notes, "Each year thousands of potentially successful businesses fail because of poor financial management. As a business owner, you will need to identify and implement policies that will lead to and ensure that you will meet your financial obligations.

"To effectively manage your finances, plan a sound, realistic budget by determining the actual amount of money needed to open your business (start-up costs) and the amount needed to keep it open (operating costs). The first step to building a sound financial plan is to devise a start-up budget. Your start-up budget will usually include such one-time-only costs as major equipment, utility deposits, down payments, etc." The SBA recommends budgeting for these expenses:

Start-up Budget

- Personnel (costs prior to opening)
- Legal/professional fees
- Occupancy

- Licenses/permits
- Equipment
- Insurance
- Supplies
- Advertising/promotions
- Salaries/wages
- Accounting
- Income
- Utilities
- Payroll expenses

The operating budget, explains the SBA, is essential when you are prepared to open those virtual Web doors. "The operating budget will reflect your priorities in terms of how you spend your money, the expenses you will incur, and how you will meet those expenses (income). Your operating budget also should include money to cover the first three to six months of operation." The SBA suggests budgeting for the following expenses:

Operating Budget

- Personnel
- Insurance
- Rent
- Depreciation
- Loan payments
- Advertising/promotion
- Legal/accounting
- Miscellaneous expenses
- Supplies
- Payroll expenses
- Salaries/wages
- Utilities

- Dues/subscriptions/fees
- Taxes
- Repairs/maintenance

In addition, the SBA recommends that the financial section of your business plan include "any loan applications you've filed, a capital equipment and supply list, balance sheet, breakeven analysis, pro forma income projections (profit and loss statement) and pro forma cash flow. The income statement and cash flow projections should include a three-year summary, detail by month for the first year, and detail by quarter for the second and third years."

Generally, this section of the business plan also addresses the accounting system and inventory control system that you will be using. Whether you develop the accounting and inventory systems yourself, have an outside financial adviser develop the systems, or just happen to have a sister-in-law who's a stellar CPA, you will need to acquire a thorough understanding of each segment and how it operates. Your financial adviser can assist you in developing this section of your business plan.

Other questions that you will need to consider are:

- What type of accounting system will you use? Is it a single-entry or dual-entry system?
- What are your sales goals and profit goals for the coming year?
- What financial projections will you need to include in your business plan?
- What kind of inventory control system will you use?

The SBA emphasizes that "your plan should include an explanation of all projections. Unless you are thoroughly familiar with financial statements, get help in preparing your cash flow and income statements and your balance sheet. Your aim is not to become a financial wizard, but to understand the financial tools well enough to gain their benefits. Your accountant or financial adviser can help you accomplish this goal." The SBA also recommends that you consider consulting your local SBA office for help with some of the more complex financial topics by checking the U.S. government section of your local telephone directory.

Other helpful resources for calculating sales, profits, advertising costs, personnel costs, and so forth include:

- Trade associations or organizations
- Your local bank
- Your public library's reference section

If you live in a city or town with a university or college nearby, you may also want to consult their library. If they have a graduate business department, for example, you may find useful information there.

Checklist

Following the advice of experts and the SBA, use this checklist to help complete the finance section. In addition to including any financial history for your company and your future projects, make sure that you include your income projection (profit and loss statement), balance sheet, and monthly cash flow projection, as summarized below. If you are unsure about any areas, consult an expert about your own situation.

Income Projection

Items typically included in this section are total net sales (revenues), controllable expenses, fixed expenses, and net profit (loss) before taxes and after taxes. This profit and loss statement should preview the amount of income generated monthly and for the year, based on your predictions of each month's sales, costs, and expenses. You will also want to include the industry percentage—a calculation of percentages of total sales (revenues) that are standard for your industry.

Balance Sheet

On your balance sheet, you should include your company's total assets, total liabilities, and total net worth (owner equity). The total assets should be equivalent to the total liabilities plus total net worth.

Monthly Cash Flow Projection

Include the cash on hand, total cash receipts, total cash available, total cash paid out, cash position, and operating details (sales volume, inventory, accounts payable, and other non-cash flow data).

11
Final Flourishes

Now is the time for all good men and women to come to the aid of their business plans. First challenge: fuhgeddaboutit!

Huh? Yup. Forget about your dot-com plan for a few days. Set it aside. Lock it into a safe and ask a friend to keep the key for a few days, if that's what it takes. But you need a break so you can get a new perspective. So try rock climbing. Or take your three-year-old to Disneyland. Or just rest in a hammock and read trashy novels. Just do something to displace your business plan in your consciousness.

Now that you're refreshed, pretend that you're a prospective investor with money burning your pockets. Does this plan give you a feeling of confidence that you'll get a return on your dollars—or does it make you feel like you might as well literally burn your dollar bills if you invest in this business? In particular, study the following.

- *The executive summary.* It's the First Encounter of the Business Kind that your reader will experience. And, although it would be lovely to think that every prospective investor reads the entire business plan, many of them review only the executive summary. Keeping in mind that the executive summary may be your one and only dot-com chance, make sure that it successfully introduces and covers every highlight and unique aspect of your plan. Are there sections that need to be elaborated on? Are certain areas too vague or rambling? Apply the business plan KISS rule: Keep It Short and Succinct.

- *The flow of the plan.* Edit yourself ruthlessly. Is your plan coherent? Is it too long in some areas (remember KISS)? Do you promise the sun, moon, and stars, and success akin to Amazon.com's—but never show concretely how you'll deliver on those promises?

> **Tip:** If you can't operate on an ailing business plan, find a qualified editor or writer who can.

APPEND THAT APPENDIX

The end is in sight—but don't write off the appendix as unnecessary. This section is both an excellent opportunity to show off items that do not necessarily fit into a traditional business plan and a final chance to leave your potential investors with a positive impression. In addition to résumés, letters of reference, and any relevant publications or press releases, you could include items ranging from samples of a product to photographs. For example, for Turnip-Chips.com, I could offer sample packages of my incredibly delicious Turnip Chips; for Grrlbiz.com, I might include letters of support for my concept from school principals, women's groups, and executives of organizations for young women and teenagers.

In other words, the elements that you should include depend on your specific business. Here is how you might design the appendix to apply to your business case.

- Include your résumé and those of your managers and/or most critical employees. For example, because the nutritional benefits of Turnip Chips are so important in the sale of the product, I would want to include the résumé and credentials of the head nutritionist and dietitian for Turnip-Chips.com.

- Provide designs, logos, sketches, and/or other illustrations that help demonstrate your product and/or show the flavor of your business.

- Attach any clips you have. Suppose I have several entrepreneurial and financial experts on the staff of Grrlbiz.com who have given lectures and written books. Both the lectures and books have received extensive coverage in the press. I would then select the best clips for inclusion in the appendix.

- Supply "testimonials" from any potential customers who have already expressed interest by sending you letters. For Turnip-Chips.com, I could include letters from health food store owners and gym executives who, after tasting Turnip Chips during the Beta program (i.e., the testing and troubleshooting program), want to purchase large quantities to sell in their stores and health clubs.

GIVE YOURSELF A TITLE

Remember when you were in college writing a report? You needed a title page. The same rule applies to your business plan. The title page should include the business plan title, the date, and your name, business address, phone number, and e-mail address.

If you have an existing Web site, include the URL—provided the site is complete enough to be an element in your favor. If your Web site is filled with Under Construction warnings, omit the URL on the title page.

TABLE TIME

The table of contents follows the executive summary. You should include all section headings and any subsections. All pages should be numbered and double-spaced, and the numbers should be included in the table of contents. Thus, if a reader finishes the executive summary and wants to jump immediately to the management section, your contents page should lead the way.

> **Red-Flag Warning:** If you choose not to hire an editor, be sure to use your word-processing program's spell checker. Guy Kawasaki of Garage.com spells out the importance of this step very succinctly: "Proofreading is important unless you want to look like a dope who can't use a spell checker."

It's essential to take the time to polish your executive summary. That section, notes Guy Kawasaki, should cover the "elevator pitch, problem solved, and background of key founders," and he cautions that potential investors study the pitch with particular care. Here's his advice on length: "A two- to three-page executive summary is all that's necessary to open the door"—and "no business plan should be more than 20 pages."

Need a refresher on the term "elevator pitch"? Then take a ride on the vocabulary cluetrain with me:

Envision yourself walking into an office building and heading toward the elevator. Out of the corner of your eye, you realize that the Greatest Investor in the World (GIW) is standing next to you. You both enter the elevator, and the doors close.

GIW presses the button for the 29th floor. You follow his lead and—buzz! You're off. You have 30 seconds (possibly less, depending on the speed of the elevator), to pitch your dot-com business. You should summarize the nature of your business (e.g. the key product or service), your target customer and why that individual will be attracted to your Web site, market potential, and sales method. Comment on the strength of your management team, and the potential for return on investment…and step gracefully off the elevator while handing GIW your business card.

DON'T JUDGE A BOOK BY ITS COVER . . . AND OTHER FINAL NOTES AND NITS

Some additional thoughts before the light shines at the end of the business plan tunnel.

• "Don't judge a book by its cover" is no lie when it comes to business plans: If you submit a plan that lacks a table of contents, was obviously copied on a xerox machine that needed new toner, is marred with typos and grammatical errors, and has a cover that consists of a piece of badly cut construction paper, it will end up where it belongs: the trash can.

You may want to use a spiral binding, and you should definitely include covers. This is not the time to try to save money by stapling your plan or using binder clips.

That might work for a high school term paper—but it won't cut the muster when it comes to impressing investors.

Be sure that you have included a clearly formatted title page and table of contents. Include your company's name, snail mail and e-mail addresses, telephone numbers, contact person, date, and copy number.

I also recommend that you add a confidentiality statement. Why a copy number and confidentiality statement? The copy number allows you to track how many copies are circulating; the confidentiality statement shows that you believe in the value of your GreatIdea-dotcom.

• Don't overlook the value of experts. This is the time when you need to be honest with yourself. Do your financial calculations make sense? Did you analyze legal considerations—or just wing them and hope the investors skip that section? Do you feel confident about your writing and editing ability—or would a proofreader come in handy?

At the very least, do ask another person to read the executive summary. Because it prefaces the table of contents, it is what prospective investors and top-level potential staff members will want to read first. Getting an outside opinion can help point out sentences and/or sections that may be clear as a blue sky to you—but bear more resemblance to a pea-soup fog to your readers.

And ask your "second opinion" person to be honest about the length of your business plan. Even if readers are interested enough when they finish reading your executive summary to keep reading, it's important to keep your business plan short and sweet. Remember: you're operating in the Internet world, where Web surfers expect byte-size blurbs, not long, pontifical pages of text. If your plan is more than 50 pages, it needs to be ruthlessly chopped (another place where an objective pair of eyes, such as an editor can provide, will come in handy).

Tip: You may want to see if you can work out a barter arrangement for an editor or proofreader. For example, I could offer to proof and edit a Web site designer's business plan in exchange for his promise to help with my Web site design.

Here's the Small Business Administration's recommendation for the final stages of planning: "Once you have completed your business plan, review it with a friend or business associate. When you feel comfortable with the content and structure, make an appointment to review and discuss it with your banker. The business plan is a flexible document that should change as your business grows."

WANT MORE TIPS, INCLUDING TIPTOEING AROUND TRAPS?

I recommend these links to assist you in completing the last elements of your business plan:

- From the CCH Business Owner's Toolkit, information about every aspect of a business plan, including "Using the Completed Plan" and "Business Plan Case Studies":

  http://www.toolkit.cch.com/text/P02_0001.asp

  In particular, read the information about the cover and table of contents:

  http://www.toolkit.cch.com/text/P02_5150.asp

  and guidance about your appendix at:

  http://www.toolkit.cch.com/text/P02_5701.asp

- From the Canada/British Columbia Business Service Centre (why is it that British spellings always look so much more elegant?), discussions of "Planning Fundamentals," including the preparation of a business plan and sample plans:

  http://www.sb.gov.bc.ca/smallbus/workshop/why-plan.html

- From BizPlanIt.com, a "virtual business plan" that includes a sample table of contents, details about every section of a business plan, and tips on what to avoid as well as what to include:

  http://www.bizplanit.com/vplan.htm

  In particular, read the section on the table of contents, which includes the basics, common errors to avoid, and sample headings:

  http://www.bizplanit.com/vplan/toc.htm

- At Bplans.com, you can find a variety of sample business plans. I recommend choosing the one that's most applicable to your own business model. Among the samples, for example, are business plans for a consulting company, a flower importer, and a software company:

  http://www.bplans.com/sample.htm

- The Small Business Administration's index to "Starting Your Business" includes everything from questions to ask yourself about becoming an entrepreneur to an outline for a business plan to financing information to a glossary of terms. (For additional dot-com-business-related terms, be sure to read the "Lexicon/Glossary" section in the Dot-Com Directory):

  http://www.sba.gov/starting/indexstartup.html

LAST, BUT NOT LEAST

Are you wondering if your business plan is grammatically correct? Worried that your writing style needs a refresher course?
    Try these Web sites:

- The Rensselaer Polytechnic Institute offers a basic guide to prose style and mechanics such as proper punctuation:

  http://www.rpi.edu/dept/llc/writecenter/web/text/pros-eman.html

- The Business Language Update Web site (which begins with my favorite Yogi Berra quote: *"The future ain't what it used to be."*) includes recommendations for style ranging from a guide to *"Gender-Neutral Writing"* to recommendations on avoiding business cliches to the *"Ten Commandments of Clarity"*:

  http://www.interlog.com/~flebo/instref.htm

- *The Elements of Style*, by William Strunk, Jr., is a classic and well worth the investment of your reading time. It includes usage rules, composition guidelines, spelling, and more:

  http://www.bartleby.com/141/index.html

- Dictionary.com also includes a link to a thesaurus. So if you look up the meaning of a word and think, "Hmmm, that's kind of it, but I think there's another term," just click the *Roget's Thesaurus* link to view other options:

  http://dictionary.com/

Checklist

Yahoo! You're almost finished and on your way to becoming just as famous as the Yahooholian executives. But first, check out this checklist:

☐ Did you review the executive summary, making sure that all sections and highlights are well covered?

☐ Have you evaluated the flow of the plan, to ensure that it moves smoothly from one section to the next?

☐ Did you include appropriate material in the appendix to your business plan?

☐ What about that title page? Does it include the business plan title, the date, your name, business address, phone number, e-mail address, and, if well-developed, your Web site URL?

☐ Is your executive summary followed by a table of contents?

☐ Are all pages numbered and double-spaced, with the numbers included in the table of contents?

☐ Did you proofread your business plan and use a spell checker? Or, if you know your weaknesses, and grammar and spelling rank high among them, did you hire an editor to review your plan?

☐ Have you protected your plan from mailing mishaps with a cover?

☐ Did you seek out others in the industry to review your plan objectively? Remember: it's difficult to see yourself as others see you—and that truth applies to your e-biz plan as well. So ask independent readers to give their views on your plan.

☐ Last, but not least: use enough postage. As one e-biz owner whom I interviewed confessed, "I had carefully chosen three venture capital firms who I thought would be perfect for my concept. I sent them my business plans—and heard nothing." Mr. Please-Keep-Me-Anonymous learned the reason when the packages boomeranged back to him. "They were all marked 'insufficient postage,' and two of the three firms apparently had just refused to pay the extra postage. At the third company, though, someone had scribbled a note on the package: 'If you're this bad at finances, don't try to be an entrepreneur.'" Final tip: ask the nice post office to weigh and stamp those packages for you.

12
Sample Business Plans

INTRODUCTION

Congratulations! If you've followed the directions in this guide, you have now created a dot-com business plan that will wow those prospective investors. Every plan is unique, as noted earlier, and you may have modified the guidelines offered here to create a business plan that showcases your concept and data. Before you delve into the Dot-Com Directory for more details on topics that interest you, however, you may want to review some examples of business plans. There are a variety available on the Web, some of which are listed below. Below that list is an executive summary for that category killer, Turnip-Chips.com; following that summary are sections from a sample business plan for Turnip-Chips.com

Some of the most detailed and accurate plans available on the Internet include:

- The Moot Corp Competition:

   http://www.brs-inc.com/plans.org/mootcorp.html

   You can choose from a list that includes competition-winning dot-com companies' business plans.

- The Canada/BC Business Service Centre:

   http://www.sb.gov.bc.ca/smallbus/workshop/sample.html

You'll find a downloadable sample business plan for a fictitious company called "Light Guard."

- Jian.com:

  http://www.jian.com/html/r_splan.asp

  A complete business plan awaits you at this site, from its title page to its conclusions.

- Bplans.com:

  http://www.bplans.com/samples/index.cfm?affiliate=bplans

  This Web site offers both start-up and established business plans and includes a "Plan Wizard" that you can use to see which sample plans would be most helpful for your particular business.

Want to Invest in Turnip Chips?

This book would not be complete without a sample business plan for the category killer of the dot-com world: Turnip-Chips.com. Below, you'll find a short business plan for that site. Although it's obviously fictional, it will give you an idea of how to fit the different pieces of your biz plan puzzle together.

TURNIP-CHIPS.COM BUSINESS PLAN

1.0 Executive Summary

Turnip-Chips.com features a product that looks and tastes like potato chips. But does the world need another potato chip brand? Well, yes. At least when it comes to a brand that is low-calorie, seasoned with anti-oxidants and other health and longevity ingredients, and a winner in a variety of taste tests throughout the nation.

In addition, Turnip-Chips.com's manufacturing features a gigantic turnip-slicer and outdoor gizmo that will bake the turnip slices with the power of the sun, thus appealing to those who seek to invest in and purchase environmentally friendly products.

One of the key features of Turnip-Chips.com's Web site is the free fitness and nutrition section, where "virtual coaches" specialize in personal fitness training and diet and nutrition counseling.

1.1 Mission Statement and Company Description

Our mission statement: "Enjoy improved health and a longer life by snacking on low-calorie, deliciously gourmet Turnip Chips. Take advantage of our free, personalized fitness and nutrition center and energize your body today!"

Turnip-Chips.com will create a unique niche: a Web site that is designed both to sell a healthy, tasty, environmentally friendly product and to educate consumers about solar energy, health, and fitness. In addition to staff experts, Turnip-Chips.com will utilize the services of solar energy groups, health and fitness groups, and other outside resources.

1.2 Management

As CEO and founder of Turnip-Chips.com, I plan to use my 12 degrees from Harvard and Yale in communications studies, management, information systems, psychology, and other relevant fields to ensure that investors' money is properly utilized. In addition to my educational background, I have served as the Chief Operating Officer for It's-a-Winner-Dot-Com; the Marketing and Sales Director for Free-Ride-to-Riches-Not-Rags-Dot-Com, and the Financial and Human Resources Vice-President for Buy-Here-Buy-Now-Buy-Early-Buy-Late-Just-Buy-Dot-Com.

I have studied Web site design extensively and plan to personally manage the position of Webmaster for that reason. Because that position is key, I also plan to hire several graphic artists/Webmasters to assist in creating and maintaining our Web site. Other members of the Turnip-Chips.com management team include:

- Gigi Button: With an MBA from UCLA and 14 years of experience as a comptroller for various dot-com companies, Ms. Button is well-qualified to serve as Turnip-Chip's Chief Financial Officer.
- Maxwell Maximum: With a background including related positions at Library-Rock-And-Roll-Dot-Com and Celebrate-Librarians-Dot-Com and a doctoral degree in business, specializing in marketing, from Princeton, Max will play a key role as Marketing and Sales Vice-President.

- Windsor Winsome: Founder of Solar Cooking Creative Inc., past president of No-Pollutants Renewable Energy Sources, Ltd., and a well-known consultant on "green" energy sources, Windsor will serve as Vice-President of Operations and Manufacturing.

- Heloise Happy: With more than seven years of experience in office administration and human resources, Heloise will take on the role of Administrative Director.

1.3 The Competition

Our research unveiled no products equal to Turnip Chips in taste and health value. Comparisons of snack foods such as fat-free potato chips with Turnip Chips, for example, showed that the potato chips fall short in the health area, since the ingredients used to reproduce the "mouth feel" of fat may cause unpleasant physical side-effects.

Moreover, Turnip Chips' low manufacturing cost will result in a product that will cost the consumer less than other functional foods, such as calcium-enhanced candy and cholesterol-lowering margarines. Usability testing revealed that Turnip Chips were viewed as highly popular, and that the name was well-received as well.

1.4 The Market/Your Customer

Targeting men and women from teens to seniors, Turnip-Chips.com is designed to appeal to health-conscious people of all ages who enjoy good food. With their nutritional value, taste appeal, and low cost, Turnip Chips is a market pleaser.

Our research (see appendix) included scientific tests that proved Turnip Chips can reduce the risk of cancer, lower the likelihood of heart disease, and improve memory.

1.5 Products/Services

As noted, Turnip Chips were fully tested for taste and nutritional benefits. As detailed in the appendix, extensive tests and analyses were run. The results were conclusive: among existing snack foods, Turnip Chips was the winner with regard to its taste and its low-calorie and beneficial qualities.

The usability group testing and limited market rollouts also substantiated the results of these tests. Several test tasters asked how they could invest in Turnip-Chips.com, so that they could, as one individual phrased it, "Put my money behind my mouth's opinions!"

Information about our environmentally aware production methods also interested and pleased consumers and the media, resulting in numerous additions to our press release list and increased visits to our preliminary Web site.

1.6 Marketing and Sales

The marketing and sales methods will include free samples of Turnip Chips at health clubs and fitness spas across the country, product demonstrators with literature and free samples in grocery stores and health stores nationwide, sales pitches to physicians, press releases and samples to health and fitness magazine editors and TV show producers, and related rollouts. We will also follow the standard procedure of submitting our site to search engines, directories, and industry publications.

We've identified our customers as primarily 21 and older, targeting individuals who are interested in improving their health and fitness. Because an increasing number of teenagers also are aware of the importance of good nutrition, they may also be attracted to the product. Although the average child will not be attracted by the product, some parents may wish to offer Turnip Chips to their children as a healthy alternative to potato chips and other snack food. However, because the youth market for Turnip Chips is less certain, initial promotional funds will not be spent on them.

1. 7 Operations

Turnip-Chips.com will require careful attention to every facet of operations and manufacturing, from the storage space to the manufacturing, packaging and delivery mechanism. Complete details are contained in the appendix.

As noted, Windsor Winsome will serve as Vice-President of Operations and Manufacturing. His experience in founding Solar Cooking Creative Inc. and helming No-Pollutants Renewable Energy Sources, Ltd. has proved invaluable in establishing the most efficient and effective methodologies for manufacturing and shipping the Turnip Chips.

Complementing Mr. Winsome's expertise is Heloise Happy's experience in office administration and human resources. Based on Ms. Happy's and Mr. Winsome's numerous contacts, we have been able to procure office and rental space in half of an underutilized manufacturing facility at below-the-market costs, including fully paid-for utilities. All executives have agreed to contribute storage space within their homes for the first year of operation, thus eliminating those costs, and the shipping concerns have been minimized by the fact that Mr. Winsome's son-in-law is the owner of Ship-A-Chip, Inc., one of the leaders in potato chip and corn chip shipping.

1.8 Financial Projections and Plans

We are fully aware of the responsibilities that we have to manage our finances in such a way that our investors will receive significant returns from their investments. Particularly advantageous to keeping our costs low are these factors:

- The low cost of manufacturing Turnip Chips, due to both the choice of solar energy and the fact that turnips are an inexpensive commodity.

- Windsor Winsome's and Heloise Happy's numerous contacts, which have resulted in office and rental space at below-the-market costs, including fully paid-for utilities.

- Agreement from every executive to contribute storage space within his or her home for the first year of operation, thus eliminating those costs.

- Minimal shipping costs, due to the fact that Mr. Winsome's son-in-law is the owner of Ship-A-Chip, Inc., one of the leaders in potato chip and corn chip shipping.

As detailed in the financial section of this plan, we have utilized the services of experienced consultants to determine the initial costs of starting Turnip-Chips.com, as well as the operating costs. Included in that section are our sales forecast, cash flow projections, projected income statements, break-even analysis, and balance sheet. As noted above, Gigi Button will serve as Chief Financial Officer, utilizing her MBA and previous experience as a dot-com comptroller.

2.0 Mission Statement and Company Description

After evaluating our mission and goals and meeting in brainstorming groups, our team has developed the following mission statement: "Enjoy improved health and a longer life by snacking on low-calorie, deliciously gourmet Turnip Chips. Take advantage of our free, personalized fitness and nutrition center and energize your body today!"

Our company has designed a unique niche. What other Web site is designed both to sell a healthy, tasty, environmentally friendly product and to educate consumers about solar energy, health, and fitness?

With regard to our product, it has been scientifically developed to be both delicious and healthful. In tandem with that development, we have called upon experts to create a manufacturing and production methodology that utilizes the latest developments in solar energy and environmentally safe standards.

Because we are utilizing both staff experts and outside resources such as solar energy groups and health and fitness groups, our site will offer a variety of opportunities to generate positive "buzz" and publicity, ranging from articles in industry magazines to talk show opportunities.

Features will include chat rooms, with scheduled talks with and by experts in different areas, free e-mail, bulletin boards, and other forums to interact with Turnip-Chips.com's community and provide growth. All messages to customer service and the company will be responded to promptly.

3.0 Management

As CEO and founder of Turnip-Chips.com, I plan to use my 12 degrees from Harvard and Yale in communications studies, management, information systems, psychology, and other relevant fields to ensure that investors' money is properly utilized. In addition to my educational background, I have served as the Chief Operating Officer for It's-a-Winner-Dot-Com; the Marketing and Sales Director for Free-Ride-to-Riches-Not-Rags-Dot-Com; and the Financial and Human Resources Vice-President for Buy-Here-Buy-Now-Buy-Early-Buy-Late-Just-Buy-Dot-Com.

I have studied Web site design extensively, and plan to personally manage the position of Webmaster for that reason. Because that position is key, I also plan to hire several graphic artists/Webmasters to assist in creating and maintaining our Web site. Other members of the Turnip-Chips.com management team include:

- Gigi Button: Gigi will serve as Chief Financial Officer. She has an MBA from UCLA and 14 years of experience as a comptroller for various dot-com companies. In addition, Gigi will advise on the company's legal issues, since she also has a law degree from UCLA' s School of Law, and help with business development. Gigi will directly supervise the accounting and payroll departments.

- Maxwell Maximum: Max will focus on marketing and sales in his role as Marketing and Sales Vice-President. His background includes related positions at Library-Rock-And-Roll-Dot-Com and Celebrate-Librarians-Dot-Com; he has a doctoral degree in business, specializing in marketing, from Princeton. Max will directly supervise the sales, marketing, customer service, and public relations departments.

- Windsor Winsome: Windsor will serve as Vice-President of Operations and Manufacturing. He founded Solar Cooking Creative Inc., subsequently sold the company and took on the position of President of No-Pollutants Renewable Energy Sources, Ltd. Windsor has degrees in environmental science and management science, has advised many cities and counties on how to convert their municipal electricity supply to renewable sources, has written seven books on "green" energy sources, and has assisted many corporations in becoming "green" facilities by utlizing wind or solar energy. Windsor will supervise all operations and manufacturing personnel, including the shipping department.

- Heloise Happy: As Administrative Director, Heloise will directly supervise the human resources and office staff. Heloise has more than seven years of experience in office administration and human resources. In addition to her corporate experience, she has degrees in health sciences and nutrition and is a certified personal fitness trainer. She therefore will play a key role in recruiting and retaining additional diet, nutrition, health, and fitness experts.

4.0 The Competition

An intensive search for snack foods that rival Turnip Chips in taste and health value revealed few, if any, contenders. For example, although manufacturers of fat-free potato chips may boast of how low calorie their offerings are, many health officials are dubious about the negative impact of the ingredients used to produce those products. And consumers certainly aren't frantically emptying the shelves of fat-free potato chips that tend to produce gas and diarrhea (not to mention their negative effect on absorption of vitamins). The fact that Turnip Chips are (a) healthy, (b) low calorie, and (c) tasty is guaranteed to be in our favor.

Another factor in our favor is the low cost of manufacturing Turnip Chips, due to both the choice of solar energy and the fact that turnips are an inexpensive commodity.

Consider Viactiv® Products, for example, which produces Viactiv Hearty Energy Bars (featuring, among other admittedly worthy ingredients such as fruit, vitamins, and minerals, sugar), Viactiv Energy Fruit Crispy Bars (a similar product), and Viactiv Soft Calcium Chews (high in calcium—and sugar). These products are expensive to manufacture and, as a result, cost the consumer more than Turnip Chips. In addition, Viactiv's products are focused at women, while Turnip Chips are destined to appeal to all ages, both male and female.

Turnip-Chips.com's competitive analysis team intensively researched health and fitness publications and Web sites, looking at the ads and product reviews, to see what similar products, if any, were advertising and/or had already achieved PR. They also visited health clubs, health food stores, and sports stores, visiting with consumers, asking their opinions on what products they enjoy for guilt-free snacking, and offering them free samples of Turnip Chips. The typical response after sampling our product: "Wow! This rivals anything I've tried. Where and when can I buy some?" Many consumers also loved the name of our site and asked if they could purchase Turnip-Chips.com T-shirts. That concept has been added to our future plans, since we want to keep our initial expenditures low until we realize a profit. The team handed out business cards and car bumper stickers advertising the site.

Some research was also done on Web sites offering fitness and nutrition information. However, since the product (Turnip Chips) rather than the service (fitness and nutrition information and help) is our main emphasis, we do not see these sites as contenders. Instead, we view them as evidence that our fitness and nutrition area, which exists to encourage consumers to return to the site and see our latest prices, new offerings, and so forth, will be popular.

5.0 The Market/Your Customer

Turnip-Chips.com's target audience consists of both men and women of all ages who are health-conscious and/or weight-conscious and want to enjoy a virtuous way to snack on delicious foods. Although teenagers and young adults are in this category, aging baby boomers also are increasingly paying attention to ways to improve their physical well-being. Because Turnip Chips are low-calorie, have "munch crunch" taste appeal, and offer multiple health benefits, they will attract consumers from ages 12 to 102.

The growing audience for functional foods will be drawn to this product, since Turnip Chips have been scientifically tested and proven to reduce the risk of cancer and heart disease and increase memory as well. Our research included interviews and sample tests at health food stores, and similar outlets, with free samples sent to editors at health and fitness publications and Web sites, inviting them to comment on and review the product. The results demonstrated that this target audience was attracted to and enjoyed Turnip Chips.

Because Turnip-Chips.com will have a fitness and nutrition advice area, it will attract and retain consumers; the product will also have a rollout that will include samples and sales in health food stores, health clubs, and sporting goods stores and may eventually lead to wholesale and retail distribution methods.

I am also fully aware of just how important customer service and customer care are on the Internet. Customers will be given the following options with regard to communicating with Turnip-Chips.com: a free 1-800 number, e-mail, and "snail mail." All phone calls and messages will be promptly answered. In addition, both on the Web site and on every package, there will be a money-back guarantee, and we will stand behind our promise.

6.0 Products/Services

As noted, Turnip Chips have been tested both with regard to their taste and health benefits. The appendix includes extensive data from the tests and analyses that were run, including comparisons to similar products, all of which demonstrated that no snack food can beat Turnip Chips in its unique low-calorie/health-improving/taste ratings. Also included are testimonies and statistics, showing how taste tests conducted across the nation and Canada proved that 99 percent of tasters preferred Turnip Chips over potato chips. We hope that you enjoyed the sample packages of Turnip Chips that accompanied this business plan; please contact us at 1-800-Turnip-Chips-Dot-Com if you would like to sample additional flavors (in addition to the original, identical-to-potato-chips flavor, we offer chive'n'sour cream, garlic, and BBQ flavored Turnip Chips and recently developed a cinnamon and sugar turnip chip that tastes, smells, and looks exactly like a delectable sugar cookie).

Also included in the appendix are photos of the attractive product, which is identical to potato chips in shape, color, size, texture, and taste, with happy and healthy customers of all ages savoring every bite!

It is worth noting that although the test markets and usability group testing showed that consumers were initially dubious when told that this product, although it looked and tasted like potato chips, was made from turnips, it took only a single bite to convince them of the validity of that statement. When followed up with documented proof of Turnip Chips' health value, the response was unanimous: "More, please!"

In this environmentally conscious age, consumers were also intrigued by and delighted in the description of the gigantic turnip-slicer and equipment that will handle every step of the production and manufacturing process fueled by the power of the sun. This aspect of our company also fueled considerable interest among editors and writers whom we contacted, and many members of the media asked to be added to the press release list.

Both consumers and media members asked if tours of the facility were available, and, as detailed in the appendix, future expansion plans include offering such tours and free samples.

As noted in the appendix, Turnip-Chips.com does own patents on all our inventions, has defined the inventory and rollout for our initial five years of operation, and has utilized experts to assist with calculating associated costs, staffing, and time commitments required for every step of production.

The fitness and nutrition expert section of the site will serve to attract the same consumers that will be interested in purchasing Turnip Chips, thus increasing sales and serving to win repeat site visitors.

7.0 Marketing and Sales

The marketing and sales methods will include free samples of Turnip Chips at health clubs and fitness spas across the country, product demonstrators with literature and free samples in grocery stores and health stores nationwide, sales pitches to physicians, press releases and samples to health and fitness magazine editors and TV show producers, and related rollouts. We will also follow the standard procedure of submitting our site to search engines, directories, and industry publications.

We've identified our customers as primarily 21 and older, targeting individuals who are interested in improving their health and fitness. Because an increasing number of teenagers also are aware of the importance of good nutrition, they may also be attracted to the product. Although the average child will not be attracted by the product, some parents may wish to offer Turnip Chips to their children as a healthy alternative to potato chips and other snack food. However, because the youth market for Turnip Chips is less certain, initial promotional funds will not be spent on them.

It is worth noting that numerous wholesalers and retailers have contacted us, due to the pre-publicity that resulted from our testing and limited market rollouts. We also have met with governmental agencies. Due to the health benefits and low production costs, there is a strong potential that turnip chips will be sold in school cafeterias and other public food locations. This arrangement strengthens our position when compared to our competitors.

Our economic consultants have analyzed factors that could potentially affect our product. They were particularly impressed with our production arrangements, which mean that any increase in energy costs will not impact our bottom line or adversely affect our costs, further strengthening our position among the competition. And, as they examined the turnip's history, they were equally pleased to learn that the turnip is the opposite of a high-priced, difficult-to-cultivate vegetable such as some of the exotic mushrooms. Indeed, turnips are one of the most common root crops and are utilized both for stock food and human food.

Thus, our goal is to create an image for Turnip-Chips.com that is ecologically astute, environmentally aware, consumer-focused, and health conscious. We seek for the highest quality in both our products and services and hope to convey that message both to our internal customers (our employees and vendors) and external customers. Combined with our extraordinarily low prices, when compared to other functional foods (such as cholesterol-lowering margarine and calcium-enriched candy), it is our firm belief that we can therefore easily stand out as the category-killer in the area of snack foods and functional/enriched foods.

8.0 Operations

Because of our resolution to be both cost-conscious and energy-efficient/environmentally aware, we have devoted ourselves to devising detailed plans for all aspects of Turnip-Chip.com's operations and manufacturing. Our staff experts, assisted by carefully selected consultants, have developed complete bluelines and project schedules for all areas, including the storage space, the production facility, the manufacturing rooms, the packaging/shipping areas, and the delivery mechanism. These bluelines, and schedules, as well as our Policies, Processes, and Procedures documents, are attached in our appendix.

Windsor Winsome, our Vice-President of Operations and Manufacturing, has succeeded in utilizing his knowledge from founding Solar Cooking Creative Inc. and helming No-Pollutants Renewable Energy Sources, Ltd. in our manufacturing methodologies. Particularly advantageous as well are his numerous contacts in the industry and government, many of whom were so intrigued by our plans that they donated their time in exchange for the opportunity to participate in such a novel concept.

Mr. Winsome and our administrative and human resources expert Heloise Happy also have succeeded in developing our office space in the most cost-efficient way. After evaluating our staff needs from start-up through the first three years, they produced spreadsheets detailing the amount of floor space needed for the initial employee head count, including the anticipated growth. They then examined studies showing the positive effect of natural sunlight (as opposed to overhead fluorescent lighting) and an "open door" policy (as opposed to the standard layout of executives-dwell-in-posh-offices-with-windows; employees-hibernate-in-tiny-cubicles-in-which-their-plants-die-due-to-the-lack-of-sunlight). A poll of executives showed that all agreed with the sentiment that caring as much for our employees as our customers will benefit the company.

Based on that consensus, Ms. Happy and Mr. Winsome were able to rent office space in half of an underutilized manufacturing facility at below-the-market costs, including fully paid-for utilities. The space is open, with numerous skylights and windows, and we plan to utilize partitions in a way that will provide all employees with natural sunlight.

Moreover, all executives are providing storage space within their homes for the first year of operation. With that cost-saving measure, and the reduced shipping costs (due to the fact that Mr. Winsome's son-in-law is the owner of Ship-A-Chip, Inc., one of the leaders in potato chip and corn chip shipping), we feel confident that our operations and productions plans are extraordinarily cost-efficient.

The appendix contains photographs, drawings, and specifications for our manufacturing mechanisms. After discussing our inventions with a patent lawyer, we have prepared a disclosure and are keeping detailed records, including renditions, of all steps involved in our inventions. As shown in the photographs, the turnip-chip-slicer is a highly refined instrument. Turnips are poured into an enormous funnel, which channels the turnips to the cleaning/scrubbing mechanism. The turnips then move rapidly along the conveyor belt (which is powered by the sun's rays) to the robotic inspector (also run on solar energy), which senses whether they pass the quality test (e.g., if they contain any dark spots, they are automatically dropped into the Make-Into-Animal-Food-Disposal-Bin). After the inspection process (three seconds per turnip), the turnip enters the sleek, impeccably clean Turnip Slicer, which slices them so thin that they are almost transluscent.

The sliced turnips are then powered along the belt to the vitamin-antioxidant-seasoning-enriched-good-for-you-most-extraordinarily-virgin-olive-oil bath, in which they reside for 1.3 minutes before baking in the solar-powered Outdoor Turnip Chip Oven.

As fully detailed in the appendix, we also investigated a variety of insurance options, vendors of equipment, materials, and supplies, Internet service providers and other Web-related items, return and guarantee policy, and security measures before finalizing every element. We are confident that in every regard, we chose the best options in terms of both cost and quality.

9.0 Financial Projections and Plans

Every aspect of our business's development has focused on providing the highest quality product for the lowest cost. For example, we are aware of such seemingly minor details as the return policy of a site and shipping costs. Surveys have shown that in order to acquire repeat customers, e-businesses must provide clear, easily accomplished return procedures and offset the shipping costs for their customers. An article in the June 12, 2000 edition of *InternetWeek* magazine, for example, cited Niha Babu, resource marketing analyst, as predicting that "the businesses that can't generate repeat customers are the ones that are going to shake out."

What makes Turnip-Chips.com unique with regard to profit are the following items:

- Our extremely low manufacturing costs, resulting from the solar energy and low cost of our main product (turnips).
- Remarkably low costs for office and rental space, with storage space provided by the executives.
- Minimal shipping costs, which mean that we can offer free standard shipping and charge only for next-day and international deliveries.

The following items are contained in the appendix:
- detailed sales forecasts
- complete cash flow projections
- projected income statements
- Turnip-Chips.com's break-even analysis
- The company's balance sheet

As noted in our pro-forma income projections, three-to-five year summary, and detailed assumptions upon which our projections are based, we have documented all assumptions with details on our budgets, known sources of funding, and marketing plans. We also have taken full advantage of all opportunities to benefit from our current investors' counseling. The management section describes the background of our administrative and operational executives, all of whom focused on establishing realistic budgets for our start-up and operating costs, which are included in the appendix.

In addition to Turnip-Chips.com's income projection statement, balance sheet, and monthly cash flow projection, the appendix provides data on three key funding sources:

- Sun Superior Inspirations Energy Systems Ltd. will pay for all start-up and operational costs for all solar-generated equipment for the first five years, in exchange for a pre-specified number of bags of Turnip Chips for its staff and a small number of stock options.
- Universe and Galactic Home and Garden Energy, Inc., has awarded Turnip-Chips.com a grant to fully fund all production and shipping

costs for the first five years of operation, in return for the display of its logo on all Turnip-Chips.com bags for the first five years.

- First and second rounds of financing from highly regarded Venture Angels & Harps Anonymous Benefactresses, who have previously funded such well-known and successful start-ups as You-Go-Girl-dotcom and Why-Reinvent-the-Wheel-dotcom.

Based on these sources of funding and cash flow projections, sales forecasts, pro-forma income projections, and related financial data, Turnip-Chips.com will realize a first-year profit of $943,712,343, as explicated in the appendix.

PART TWO

THE DIRECTORY

THE OVERVIEW

Want to know where to find statistics on how many teenagers have their own Visa cards? Looking for a business partner or financial consultant? Maybe you need graphics for your Web site.

Turn on your computer, connect to the Internet, and a few clicks will take you to…well, it depends on where you start your search. The information that you find may be useful – or it could be useless, or, even worse, downright misleading and erroneous.

And that's where this directory comes in. This directory offers a quick and easy way to find the top resources. After all, why subject yourself to carpal tunnel syndrome from hunting and clicking far and wide in the Internet realm when you can have the details at your fingertips! Included in this directory is:

- detailed information on what types of resources are available, including online government agencies, organizations, publications, and newsgroups
- useful Web sites in a variety of areas, from associations and organizations to online publications to information for young entrepreneurs (and those who are young at heart!)

BEST-BET WEB SITES

The most difficult part of creating this section was narrowing down the list. It seems as if new business-related Web sites are multiplying faster than you can say "dot-com," and many of them are excellent. The following list, therefore, represents what is admittedly my opinionated view of sites representing the cream of the dot-com crop:

- Need a break? Visit the Idea Café for everything from details on financing your business to forums to advice from experts:

  http://www.ideacafe.com/
- BizProWeb is an all-in-one site for small business owners and entrepreneurs. From newsgroups to shareware to a long list of excellent links, this site is one to bookmark:

  http://www.bizproweb.com/

- CCH Business Owner's Toolkit has a wealth of resources for small businesses, including planning assistance, management help, and marketing tips:

  http://www.toolkit.cch.com/

- AllBusiness.com describes itself as offering "solutions for growing businesses," and it lives up to that description. There's a finance center, technology information, numerous articles for entrepreneurs, and an extensive selection of useful links:

  http://www.allbusiness.com/homepage/index.asp

- You'll want to return often to Internet.com, where you can find everything from the latest e-news to marketing resources to…well, your only problem will be limiting your time browsing this site:

  http://www.internet.com/

  In particular, I recommend their e-commerce guide:

  http://ecommerce.internet.com/

- American Express has some helpful freebies. At the link below, click the Business Services link in the Small Business section:

  http://www.americanexpress.com/homepage/home.shtml

- The cliché says that "less is more," but more can be good when you need information on starting your business, running your business, tools for creating your Web site, and the latest business news. Morebusiness.com has all that, plus (need I say it?) more:

  http://www.morebusiness.com/

- Smallbizsearch.com bills itself as the place to go for "Smart Searches for Small Business." But you can do more than just conduct a standard search at this site. It's nicely organized into Web Business Guides ranging from computers to the Internet to sales to, well, check it out for yourself:

  http://www.smallbizsearch.com/

- The Entrepreneurial Edge Web site will give you an edge on the competition (Figure 1). Described as a "peer-learning community for growing communities," it contains tried-and-true links and a variety of resources:

  http://edge.lowe.org/

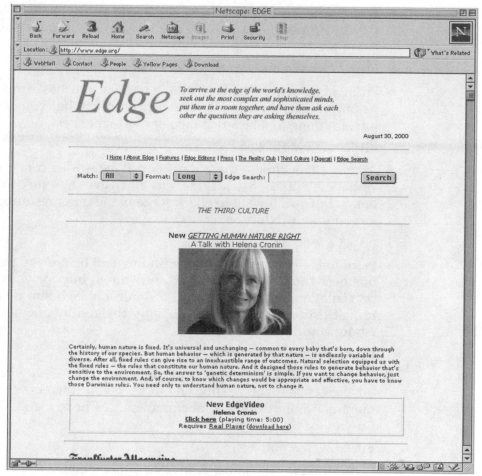

Figure 1. Click here if you want the edge on the entrepreneurial scene.

- Presented by the Kauffman Center for Entrepreneurial Research, EntreWorld's features include the latest IPO news, assistance with growing your business, a list of "hot links" for entrepreneurs, and glossaries both for computing terms and business terms:

  http://www.entreworld.org/

- Netscape's business section is not too busy, not too sparse, in short, like the porridge that Goldilocks lusted after, just right. Lots of info both on small business and personal finance in general:

  http://business.netscape.com/business/main.tmpl

- When you can't seem to find what you want, check SOHO (Small Office/Home Office). Among my favorite features on this site is the list of links:

  http://www.soho.org/reference/window.html

- From templates to tools to tips, Quicken.com has some great free resources. Yes, there is a link to their products, but you don't have to buy anything to take advantage of this great site:

  http://www.quicken.com/small_business/

- All biz, all the time—that's the scoop at the All-Biz.com Web site. The "business zones" list includes an extensive area just for entrepreneurs, but you'll want to check some of the other resources, depending on your product or service:

  http://www.all-biz.com/

- Want to know about the weather in England before you pack for your business trip? Wondering what software to buy for your marketing presentation? Hunting around for info on Web site design? If the topic exists on the 'Net, it's probably covered by one of the areas in About.com:

  http://www.about.com/

- You're wonderfully honest, forthright, and true—but what about the businesses that you're choosing to keep your own biz going? Not to mention your customers, ahem, ahem…. Check the Better Business Bureau for the scoop:

  http://www.bbb.org/

- WebData.com's business & investments section is an all-in-one stop for business financing, marketing, tools, charts, and more:

  http://www.webdata.com/pnum/Classification2.htf

UNCLE SAM CAN SOLVE YOUR PROBLEMS— WELL, SOME OF THEM...

Well, the Internet wasn't exactly invented by Al Gore. But the federal government has hyperlinked itself in a variety of areas that are useful to dot-com entrepreneurs. In addition to the Small Business Administration's home page at www.sba.gov, these sites can aid an enterprising entrepreneur.

G Is for General, B Is for Business, and...

- You can find a complete listing of the official federal government sites, courtesy of the Library of Congress' Internet Resource page, at:

  http://lcweb.loc.gov/global/executive/fed.html

  and an information locator for the government at:

  http://www.gsa.gov/

- The U.S. Department of Commerce has information on statistics, opportunities for small businesses, and more. A good way to locate what you're seeking is to go directly to its Resources page:

  http://204.193.246.62/public.nsf/docs/resources

- You'll also find statistics at Fedstats:

  http://www.fedstats.gov/

- The United States Business Advisor describes itself as a "one-stop electronic link to government for business," and it contains a frequently asked questions section, business tools and guides, a thorough search engine, and the latest business news:

  http://www.business.gov/

- Work is the buzz at the U.S. Department of Labor's Web site. A particularly excellent resource is their Office of Small Business Programs (Figure 2):

  http://www.dol.gov/dol/osbp/welcome.html

  On that site, you should also check out the Occupational Safety & Health Administration:

  http://www.osha.gov/

  and Workforce Initiatives links:

  http://www.doleta.gov/programs/onet/links.htm

- The Federal Trade Commission has a business guidance section, as well as other biz-related links:

  http://www.ftc.gov/

- The United States Census Bureau, including economic surveys and state-specific details, is useful for marketing research:

  http://www.census.gov

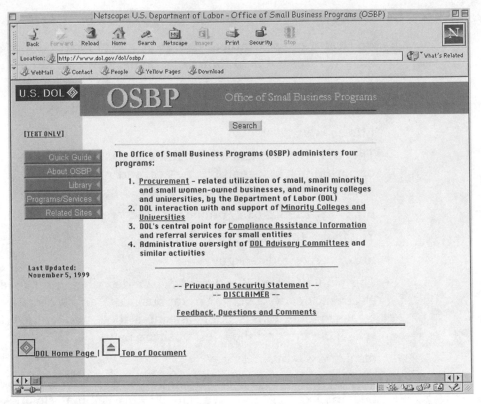

Figure 2. Don't worry: it's not as complex as the IRS, and these governmental rules and regulations are essential knowledge for your business.

- The United States Treasury encompasses a variety of offices, including everyone's favorite acronym, the IRS:

  http://www.ustreas.gov/

- Depending on your product, you may also want to check out the U.S. Trade and Development Agency:

  http://www.tda.gov/

- And last, but by no means least, remember that when in doubt, the Small Business Administration's well-designed Web site contains a wealth of resources (Figure 3):

  http://www.sbaonline.sba.gov/

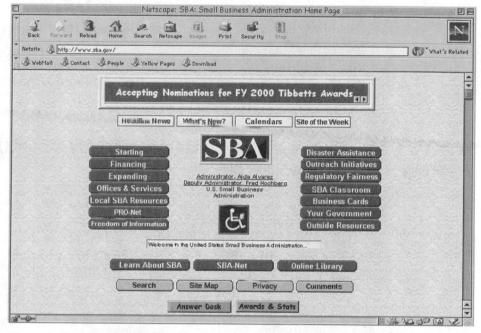

Figure 3. Familiarize yourself with this tips-, tricks-, and techniques-packed site.

At that site, be sure to visit the SBA's "Classroom," where you'll find links to an excellent array of business tools and both government and outside resources:

http://classroom.sba.gov/

Be a Local Yokel

Don't forget to check out your state's resources. You'll find Small Business Development Centers (SBDC), for example, offer a wealth of information. Co-sponsored by the SBA, they offer training programs, helpful materials, and resources for your area.

Depending on the state in which you live, you may also find useful information on its home page. For example, I live in California, where the California Secretary of State Web site includes a thorough section on business programs:

http://www.ss.ca.gov/business/business.htm

For links to a directory of SBDCs and other local, state, and government agencies, I recommend Yahoo's Small Business Information section on government agencies:

http://dir.yahoo.com/Business_and_Economy/Small_Business_ Information/Government_Agencies/

A LITTLE LIGHT READING: ONLINE AND PRINT PUBLICATIONS

Remember when your first-grade teacher solemnly intoned, "Never underestimate the value of reading"? Oh, yeah.

Well, give that teacher a brightly polished apple, because she was right. Keeping up with industry publications can help keep you informed about the latest trends, your competition, and new technology. So don't delay—subscribe today!

Tip: In addition to maintaining online versions of their print publications, some of the sites listed here provide free newsletters. Many of these publications offer free newsletters and excellent Web versions. Sample them all—then choose which ones you want to subscribe to the old-fashioned way.

- *Fast Company* is the talk of the techie town. Brash, bold, and brilliant, this magazine contains an intriguing blend of e-commerce news, entrepreneurial notes, and what might be called philosophy for the new economy. Career and personal development, management topics, and big ideas for the big picture make this online and print publication lively reading:

  http://www.fastcompany.com/homepage/

- *Entrepreneur* magazine describes itself as "the online small business authority," and if you visit the Web site (and read the print version), you'll see why. From marketing to management, start-up help to expansion details, it's one of your best bets for small business issues:

  http://www.entrepreneurmag.com/

- B is for business, and *Business2.0* is for those interested in business beyond the basics. It is the age of the Internet, of e-commerce, and of new business philosophies—and *Business2.0* doesn't play games. Particularly well-done are the articles about marketing, wheelin' and dealin' in the high-tech world, and e-biz buzz:

  http://www.business2.com/

- *Inc.* magazine is an amazingly generous publication in terms of what it offers on the Internet. In addition to the standard articles-from-the-magazine and article archive, *Inc.* features "special mini sites" that range from business technology to finance to doing business online:

  http://www.inc.com/

- *InfoWorld* may not be as lively reading as some of the other publications listed here. But its thorough coverage of information technology makes it a publication that you—or someone on your staff—should be reading:

  http://www.infoworld.com/

- *Industry Standard* is sometimes a tad dry – but its focus on e-commerce, the Internet, and cutting-edge business topics make it worth your time. Don't miss the "metrics" section for your research and statistics needs:

  http://thestandard.net/

- Pardon the pun, but *Fortune* magazine can help you make your fortune. Read the articles—and then scroll down to the Fortune Small Business link to check out "the information you need all the time":

  http://www.pathfinder.com/fortune/

- Recently, I was at the gym, doing my usual workout (grimly stepping away on the Stairmaster, magazines propped before me so that I could learn while I burned). A gym buddy glanced over my shoulder and groaned. "*Forbes* magazine! That looks like something my grandfather would read." Well, maybe. But it's not just for Grandpa anymore. The online version of *Forbes* includes a small business center that pays particular attention to the needs of e-biz entrepreneurs:

  http://www.forbes.com/tool/smallbus

- *Red Herring* might sound like a fishy name for a publication, but the e-commerce news and Internet buzz that it delivers is fresh and entertaining:

  http://www.redherring.com/

- *Upside Today* calls itself the "Tech Insider," and it features articles on the people, places, and products that are on the edge of the cutting edge: http://www.upside.com/

AND THE SEARCH IS ON

There are times when you just gotta search for it—and when that time comes, I recommend starting with one of these sites.

- AskJeeves features an intuitive and fast interface. Just enter your question in the box, and click Ask! Jeeves can even check your spelling for you. You'll get results from different search engines and directories. For example, I entered the question "How do I get financing for my new business?" The answers ranged from the not-so-useful (a definition of the term financing) to off-target (information on 52-week highs) to right-on (Small Business Financing). Give them an "A" for their ease-of-use and speed—and a "B" for results:

  www.askjeeves.com

- WebData is a newcomer to the search scene. Variety and wealth of resources are the key features to this richly textured site. Pick a subject from Arts & Humanities to Government to Telecom & Internet, and click. You'll find yourself facing a list of available databases, which in turn lead to more links. They deserve a "B" for ease of use (it takes a while to figure out how to return to the Home page) and a "B+" for variety:

  www.webdata.com

- Yahoo! is the grandparent of them all. This fully developed and beautifully designed directory still reigns as the uber-destination when it comes to your initial search. Gotta give those folks a double A:

  www.yahoo.com

- Searching for search tips (Figure 4)? Wondering if you can conduct a specialized search for your particular product (for example, if you focus on products for children, you might appreciate a special search engine that focuses on kids)? Searchability is a guide to specialized search engines. It includes descriptions for each type of search engine, and links as well:

  http://www.searchability.com/index.htm

- In contrast, 4anything (4anything.com) is focused on categories. Some are standard (including business, health, and travel), and others are a tad more nonstandard (Cities, for example, includes 4New York, 4Houston, etc.). This site's 4you if you like having shopping options mixed in with information. Thus far, they get an "A-" for ease of use and a "B" for usefulness.

- And you thought Uncle Sam was clueless? Hah! Check out the government's "Searching the Internet" guide. From a tutorial to links to some of the best search engines, this is a great beginning place for a search:

    http://www.alw.nih.gov/WWW/searching.html

- AltaVista is often mentioned when people are asked to name their favorite search engines. In addition to searching both Web sites and

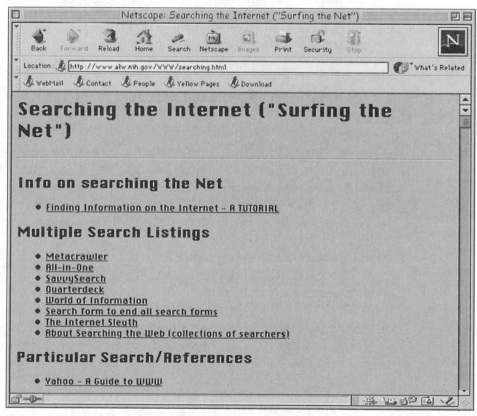

Figure 4. Your tax dollars help pay for this search engine.

Usenet newsgroups, its categories are nicely organized and make it easy to find useful information quickly:

http://www.altavista.com/

- Several entrepreneurs with whom I spoke insisted that HotBot was the best. You can customize it easily, limiting your search both efficiently and effectively:

  http://www.hotbot.com/

- If you're interested in searching newsgroups rather than the Internet, focus your search with DejaNews:

  http://www.dejanews.com

- In addition to the more general search engines, you can search specifically for business topics at these specialized sites:

  Smallbizplanet.com: http://www.smallbizplanet.com/index.html

  Smallbizsearch.com: http://www.smallbizsearch.com/

  Sookoo.com: http://www.sookoo.com/

DOES THE "E" IN E-COMMERCE STAND FOR EASY?

Alas, no. But you can make the electronic commerce aspect of your dot-com business easier by becoming alert to the many facets of this area. Taking security precautions, observing proper netiquette, avoiding those kiss-of-death-publicity site outages…the more you know, the more you'll realize how essential it is to understand e-commerce. And you'll also realize that there's no "graduation": one of the trickiest elements of the e-commerce game is that it's constantly changing.

The good news: online e-commerce resources are proliferating. Here are some worth viewing:

- PriceWaterHouseCoopers' Global Web site is an international professional services organization—and one of the organization's areas of expertise is e-business. You can view the most recent results of their venture capital survey, which is one of the most reputable available, at their site, and locate information on everything e-commerce-related from tax laws to online customer service:

  http://pwcglobal.com/

- Internet.com's Electronic Commerce Guide is a superbly designed portal to All Things Great And Small in E-biz Land. From the latest e-biz news to product reviews to downloads, this site is worth repeated visits:

  http://ecommerce.internet.com/

- CommerceNet also deserves a place in your e-commerce Bookmark collection. This international, nonprofit membership organization mission is "to promote and advance interoperable electronic com merce to support emerging communities of commerce." You don't have to be a member to utilize this Web site, however, which includes online resources, a variety of e-commerce materials, and a newsletter:

  http://www.commerce.net/

- What's the latest e-biz news? Which sites practice the best Web design and implementation? What are the latest solutions and products? The full-of-e-biz-features ZDNet + E-Business Home offers all these features—and more:

  http://www.zdnet.com/enterprise/e-business/

  and don't miss the current lists of Best and Worst E-Commerce Implementations: you'll want to study what succeeds—and what fails miserably:

  http://www.zdnet.com/enterprise/e-business/bphome/

- EMarketer's slogan is: "Where business begins online." Want e-news? They've got it. Want e-statistics? Ditto. Want dot-com company research info? Yup, emarketer.com has links for those as well.

  http://www.emarketer.com/

- The NetBusiness Web site, from CMP Net, is another site that you'll want to return to. It contains the latest electronic commerce news, excellent resources (including links specifically for small businesses), and a "clinic" serviced by Dr. Commerce. The good Doctor offers answers to questions ranging from understanding bandwith to audioconferencing details:

  http://www.techweb.com/netbiz/

- *PC Magazine*'s Top 100 Web sites are worth checking. Depending on your specific e-commerce needs, you might want to check not only the e-commerce section of sites but also the computing sites, computing stores, and Web development sections:

  http://www.zdnet.com/pcmag/special/web100/

- Security, security, security (Figure 5). From viruses to hackers to reassuring your customers that their online transactions are secure to…well, let's just say it would take another book to cover this topic. Here are a few sites to get you started on what should be an ongoing awareness of the need for security precautions. Also, be sure to check out CNET.com's security section (see below):

  - A good basic introduction is available at PGP's site:

    http://www.nai.com/asp_set/products/tns/intro.asp

  - McAfee.com covers every aspect of security for your PC, including the broader picture for your e-commerce biz:

    http://www.mcafee.com/

  - The government comes through with an excellent list of resources devoted to security:

    http://www.alw.nih.gov/Security/security.html

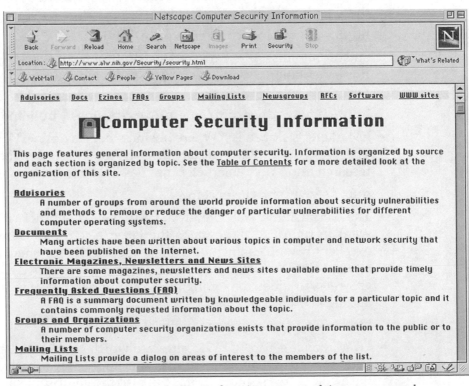

Figure 5. Security is an area that's worth an investment of time, money, and resources—and this site can get you started on what should be an ongoing concern and consideration.

- Coupled with concerns about security should be the issue of privacy. Not just for you and your employees, but for customers. Surveys have shown that many consumers hesitate to buy online because they are worried about the potential for loss of their privacy. They wonder, for example, if their e-mail address, social security number, and other personal data will be revealed to unscrupulous hackers during their transactions. To understand this situation from your customers' viewpoint and also learn what you can do to ease their worries, visit the Better Business Bureau's special Web area on e-commerce issues. It includes an area for consumers and information for businesses that includes details on how you can apply for Privacy and Reliability Seals:

  http://www.bbbonline.com/

- Two other sites that focus on privacy issues are the Electronic Privacy Information Center (http://www.epic.org/) and TRUSTe (http://www.truste.org/).

- For All Things Great and Small for your e-commerce needs, start from CNET.com's home page, and then choose the category of your choice. The Business Computing section includes resources specifically for e-business, security, and Web development; the Web Building section can simplify and streamline your Web construction efforts; the Internet section is another worth-visiting click, and you'll want to return to the home page when you're in need of reliable reviews for hardware and software items:

  http://home.cnet.com/

- AllBusiness.com's Internet section focuses on the full gambit of topics essential for e-commerce concerns, from Internet access and hosting to security to intranets and beyond. In addition to the tools link below, you can click the tabs for e-commerce-related Q&A, advice from experts, and more:

  http://www.allbusiness.com/business_center/internet/tools.asp

DANCING THE MANAGEMENT MINUET

Ah, the magic of becoming a manager! Empowered to hire and fire, to dictate policy, to determine a company's future, to…sheesh, that's a lot of responsibility!

But don't be intimidated. By hiring the best, establishing a reputation as a fair and considerate employer, consulting management experts as needed, and staying in touch with what really counts in life (friends and family), you can waltz through the management minuet gracefully.

For tips and tools, check out these resources:

- Quicken.com's section on Managing Your Business in the Small Business area of the site offers help on project management as well as general management articles and information:

  http://www.quicken.com/small_business/managing_your_business/

- The Curious Cat Management Improvement site will make you purr with satisfaction at the useful links related to management tactics:

  http://www.curiouscat.com/guides/onlineq.htm

- Inc. Online not only has a daily management tip, but it also contains a nice variety of management-related articles:

  http://www.inc.com/

- The Forbes Small Business Center is designed for biz managers and owners. You'll find a variety of articles on topics such as "Painless Perks" (defined as: how to hire good employees when you can't afford to pay the biggest bucks):

  http://www.forbes.com/tool/smallbus/

- Ever wondered just what makes a good manager? Here's an interesting article on that subject:

  http://www.thepargroup.com/managers.html

- The U.S. Business Advisor's section on Workplace Issues (Figure 6) contains help on everything from finding skilled workers to employee benefits:

  http://www.business.gov/busadv/maincat.cfm?catid=23

- In search of good employees? First, ask your employees to recommend people. And offer recruitment "bounties" when you hire someone who proves to be a winner via an employee's recommendation. Second, try posting your job on one of Go2NetNetwork's list of the 100 most popular job sites. From general (Monster.com) to specific (engineeringjobs.com), you can find a site that's right for your needs:

  http://www.100hot.com/directory/business/jobs.html

- MIT's Sloan Management Review is useful (although somewhat academic) reading for managers in all areas:

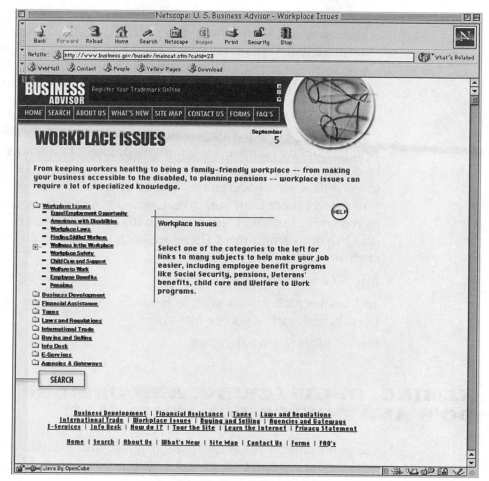

Figure 6. Never underestimate the importance of your employees—finding them and keeping them happy has become increasingly difficult, even for the most successful companies.

http://mitsloan.mit.edu/smr/index.html

- Avoid the "t" word (turnover) by becoming a snoop. Retain your employees by checking out to see what other companies offer in terms of incentives. From free on-site massages to bagels and gourmet coffee—free, of course,—every morning to a yearly percentage of stock options, the perks offered to e-biz employees are becoming legendary. Your employees will want to stay if you can equal (or better, beat) the competition. So visit the job sections on other companies' Web sites. And don't forget the straight-forward approach: ask your employees what they'd like. The answer may surprise you. One manager, for example, conducted an anonymous survey—and the most frequent request was "give us free donuts instead of granola bars." That request actually resulted in a cost-savings. And the second most frequently requested item (flex time, so that employees could start earlier or later and end their days accordingly) cost nothing—and proved easy to implement.

- And last but by no means least, in my opinion: be a leader who gives back what he or she has received. There are numerous opportunities to volunteer for a good cause. The odds are high that you'll feel as if you receive more than you give. Consider involving your employees as well (for example, volunteering with a group for a Saturday work-day in your community).There are both international organizations, such as Habitat for Humanity:

http://www.habitat.org/

and local organizations, such as Santa Clara's volunteer Web site, that need bright, caring people like you:

www.volunteerexchange.org

NAMING, REGISTERING, AND DESIGNING DO'S AND DON'T'S FOR YOUR SITE

Have you named your site yet? Registered your domain name? If not, skip down to that section now. Choosing the right name is definitely part of the e-biz game.

If you've accomplished those steps, start contemplating the issue of Web site design. Whether you plan to design your dot-com site yourself, or hire a Web site designer, or outsource it, understanding the basics of Web site design is an essential part of e-commerce. Study your competition's Web sites; analyze the Web sites of award-winning e-businesses, and figure out what separates the winners from the losers. And don't forget to seek opinions from those who count: your customers. Usability testing, even if it's informal ("Hey, best friend who's known for her honesty, tell me, what do you think of my site?"), plays an important role in creating a successful (i.e., profitable) Web site.

Naming and Registering Your Site

- Unless your name is Oprah, you may need to take some time to figure out a memorable domain name. Ask friends, relatives, and the
  clerk at the store what they think of your prospective domain name.

  I should note, though, that some e-commerce folks disagree on
  the true importance of your Web site's name. Recently, for example, I
  listened (well, okay, I kind of eavesdropped, but it was in a public
  restaurant) to this exchange between the marketing and sales vice-
  president and the Webmaster of a thriving Internet company in the
  Silicon Valley:

  "A catchy Web site name is essential. It's gotta convey the product or service that the site sells, and do it in a way that attracts attention and is memorable," insisted the Webmaster.

  "Hah!" said the VP. "What are the names of the Web sites that
  you visit the most often? Don't think about it, just spit out the four
  sites you visit most frequently."

  "Well," said the Webmaster, "Google.com, because it's a great
  search engine; tucows.com, because it's the best place to go for good
  shareware and I like their ratings; happypuppy.com, because I like
  their games section; and Amazon.com, because their prices are usually the lowest."

  The Webmaster paused a moment, then reluctantly admitted,
  "Yeah, I see what you mean: Google, Tucows, Happypuppy, and
  Amazon—none of them are really names that, if you just hear them,
  you're going to know what the product is." He cheered up.

  "But they're memorable – well, kind of."

  In other words, don't put so much effort into trying to select the
  perfect name that it's time to start preparing for Y3K before you've
  come up with the "right" one.

- After you've got your site name chosen, you need to register it. There
  are a number of sites that you can use to register your domain name.
  Register.com is one of them:

  http://www.register.com/

  and Network Solutions is another:

  http://www.networksolutions.com/

- What if you keep entering different names—and they're all taken? Sorry, Charlie, but if ILoveTuna is already registered, you need to keep seeking for another fishy name in the Web sea. A helpful article on choosing a domain name can be found on SmallOffice.com:

  http://www.smalloffice.com/sbc/101999/yrs01.htm

- There's a hot debate about whether it's worth obtaining a registered trademark for your domain site name. For details on what's involved, visit the U.S. Patent and Trademark Office (Figure 7):

  http://www.uspto.gov/

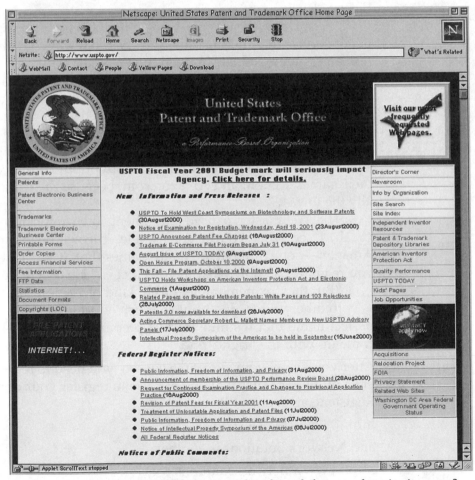

Figure 7. Considering obtaining a registered trademark for your domain site name? Here's the place with the answers.

Web Site Design

- UseIt.com focuses on "usable information technology." Of particular interest to would-be-outstanding Web site designers are the articles on subjects such as "top ten mistakes of Web design." Web site usability is a hot topic on this site, and the articles are well-written and thoroughly researched:

  http://www.useit.com/

- Hop over to Webmonkey, and your own problem will be choosing which link to click first. From the Quick Reference section (I like the HTML Cheatsheet) to tutorials on trendy topics such as animation to how-to libraries for dot-com doers, this site is definitely one to bookmark:

  http://www.hotwired.com/webmonkey/

- Internet.com's many features include a Web Reference section (http://www.webreference.com/). The Web Developer channel focuses on Web site development, design, and maintenance issues:

  http://www.internet.com/sections/webdev.html

  But if you don't want to design it yourself...Internet.com also offers a list of Web site designers that you can search through:

  http://designlist.internet.com/

- When I read about a site that has a loooong name to be typed in, I usually hesitate. But I kept coming across the "Designing a Business Web Site" URL in different articles. And when a helpful Webmaster friend sent me the URL in response to my request for the best Web design sites, I clicked it. Trust me: it's worth your time to type in this URL. From a professional Internet services company, this guide to Web design for e-businesses has a wealth of resources:

  http://www.wilsonweb.com/webmarket/design.htm

- When my Webmaster buddy sent me the BigNoseBird.com address, though, I thought he was joking. "Very funny!" I responded. "I'm serious," he said. And thus I clicked the link—and was rewarded. It's a clever name—and the concepts live up to that creativity. The site's "stuff" includes freebies, design tips and tricks, a reference section, and more:

  http://www.bignosebird.com/

- At CNET.com, start by clicking on the Web Building section, and then check out the hardware, software, and Internet sections for related help:

  www.cnet.com

- The EBoz! Web site isn't for bozos. It describes itself as "Your Guide to Creating Successful Web sites," and the contents range from a directory of resources for Webmasters to articles about Web design to Web tools:

  http://www.eboz.com/index.shtml

OF DOLLARS, INCUBATORS, AND GARAGES

This section covers the financial aspect of your business, separated into three categories:

- General Finance: You'll find information that is relevant both now (in the just-starting-out stages of your business) and later (as your e-biz becomes a growing, thriving enterprise).

- Finding Financing: This area covers the various methods of securing financing for your business. Although most of the publicity these days seems to focus on Venture Capital firms and "angel" investors, the reality is that most businesses travel other paths to locate financing. The Web sites described in this section will help you learn about your options, which range from banks to the government to "incubators" and more.

- Venture Capital Firms and Angel Investors: There's gold in them thar hills—Sand Hill, that is, one of the main regions for venture capital firms. In this section, you'll discover the pros, the cons, the whims, and the ways of VCs and angels.

And now, may the dollars flow in your direction as you begin your search:

General Finance

From magazines that will help with your personal financial needs to sites that report on the competition's financial state, online resources for your general financial needs abound.

- Describing itself as "Your Financial Strategy Center," Money.com contains links to resources and articles about investing, insurance, taxes, the market, and more:

  www.money.com

- Here's another bonus from Uncle Sam: the U.S. Securities and Exchange Commission (SEC) is home to some extremely useful Web pages, including information specifically for small businesses and the EDGAR database (Figure 8). Who the heck is EDGAR, you ask, and what did he do to deserve to have his name in capital letters? The Electronic Data Gathering, Analysis, and Retrieval system, affectionately known as EDGAR, performs automated collection, validation, indexing, acceptance, and submission forwarding by companies and others required by law to file forms with the SEC. The site also contains non-Edgar documents.

  http://www.sec.gov/index.html

Figure 8. Forget about Elvis: Maybe Edgar doesn't have blue suede shoes, but this Web site has information that's a lot more useful to entrepreneurs than memorizing some song about a hound dog.

- CNNfn, the financial network online, is a great resource for the latest financial news, information about market activity, financial articles for small businesses, and finance-related links:

  http://www.cnnfn.com/

- I can describe the Dow Jones Web site more concisely by saying what it doesn't have: no reviews of raspberry jelly donuts, no information about how to train a baby alligator to push a baby stroller, and nary a word about how many earrings can dangle from one earlobe without causing a serious case of drooping lobes. Other than those limits, the site has everything from personal finance to small business information to travel information to..., well, let's just say it's worth a visit:

  http://www.dowjones.com

Finding Financing

Show me the money...please? Sorry, Charlie. Even if you remember to say "please" and "thank you," locating financing for your dot-com business may not be the easiest game in town. That's the bad news. The good news is that there is a virtual wealth of online resources to help you:

- The Service Corps of Retired Executives (SCORE) is a good first stop. This nonprofit association has been a resource partner with the U.S. Small Business Administration for more than three decades. You can get e-mail counseling, locate a variety of financial resources, and find a local chapter that can help you with your financing questions as well:

  www.score.org

- The SBA rates high on my list, as well, for its detailed, clear explanations of your financing options. Don't skip the "related information" links:

  http://www.sba.gov/financing/

- Small Business Development Centers (SBDC) are administered and funded by the SBA, and they provide information about various aspects of starting your business, including locating financing. To locate an SBDC in your area, check this site:

  http://sbdcnet.utsa.edu/sbdc.htm

- The financial section of the Entrepreneurs' Help Page contains articles and links ranging from a discussion of obtaining funding to venture capitals to the SEC to bank loans. There's also a good list of additional resources:

  http://www.tannedfeet.com/html/financial.htm

- The National Business Incubation Association is an excellent resource for any entrepreneur considering that option. You'll get assistance with your financing, management help, shared resources, and more·

  http://www.nbia.org

- *Fortune* magazine wants to help you make your fortune by providing an excellent list of resources for finding financing:

  http://www.pathfinder.com/yourco/resources/

  http://www.pathfinder.com/yourco/resources/index.html

- American Express also offers information that will help you understand your funding options:

  http://www6.americanexpress.com/smallbusiness/resources/expanding/financing/

- Hungry for financing help? Then visit Idea Café's financing buffet, where the menu includes some suggestions for "creative" financing:

  http://www.ideacafe.com/getmoney/FINANCING.shtml

- If you can't seem to find what you want, then it's time to hunt. That task is eased by Smallbizsearch.com. But before you start a search, check out the site's great finance guide:

  http://www.smallbizsearch.com/finance/

- And another useful "I still can't find what I want" resource is the "Funding Resources on the Web" site:

  http://www.westward.com/library/cashwebs.htm

Venture Capital Firms and Angel Investors

Don't bother dreaming about the Golden Gates of San Francisco if you're an entrepreneur-in-search-of-startup-funding. Increasingly, the place to be is Sand Hill Road, where some of the most high-profile and prestigious venture capital firms have settled down to seed the Silicon Valley's fledglings. Known by some as "Fraternity Row," the region also includes various private investors (a.k.a. "angels") and related firms.

However, you definitely do not need to live in this area or plan to start up your business in earthquake country in order to qualify for funding from a VC firm or angel.

For details about just how you can get your share of the VC/angel pie, follow these links:

- The National Venture Capital Association (NVCA) is a good place to start if you want to learn more about just what venture capital funding is, and how it works (Figure 9):

  http://www.nvca.org/

- The Venture Capital Resource Library simplifies your search with its superb list of links to venture capital, angel investors, and more:

  http://www.vfinance.com/

- Both amusing and helpful, the online site for *Fortune* magazine has a series on how to impress a venture capitalist:

  http://www.pathfinder.com/yourco/articles/0,2227,218,00.html

- ACE-Net has a special section for entrepreneurs, where you'll learn more about just how an "angel" can help you. The Angel Capital Electronic Network (hence the site name, ACE-Net) is sponsored by the SBA's Office of Advocacy, and the site includes extensive information about taxes, legal issues, and related government matters as well:

  http://ace-net.sr.unh.edu/pub/

- Can Heaven exist side by side with a garage? Yes, if the "Heaven" in question has www.garage.com as its address (Figure 10). From the latest industry news to forums to research links to details about the famous company whose slogan is: "We start up startups," this site deserves a visit:

  http://www.garage.com

- Most of the major venture capital firms have their own Web sites as well, and you can often find helpful information on their pages. My favorite directory of VC firms is part of the Venture Capital Resource Library:

  http://www.vfinance.com/ventcap.htm

  For example, Idealab at http://www.idealab.com/, Hummer Winblad Venture Partners at http://www.humwin.com, Kleiner, Perkins, Caufield & Byers at http://www.kpcb.com/, Menlo

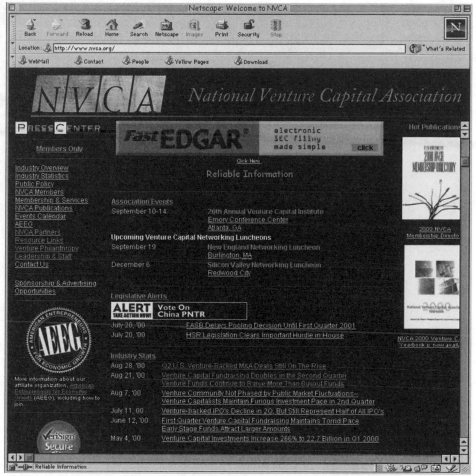

Figure 9. The newspapers print elaborate details about data and dollars flowing from venture capital firms—but it's not easy to find the basic information. This useful site spells it out.

Ventures at http://www.menloventures.com/, and Sequoia Capital at http://www.sequoiacap.com/index.html have useful details for entrepreneurs on their Web pages.

• If you want to focus on venture capital firms, I also recommend reading and following the industry publications. You can learn about individual VCs, and get an idea of what types of technology each one is interested in funding. Red Herring is one of the best (see the Dotcom Directory on publications for more), with a special section just for VC topics:

http://www.redherring.com/vc/home.html

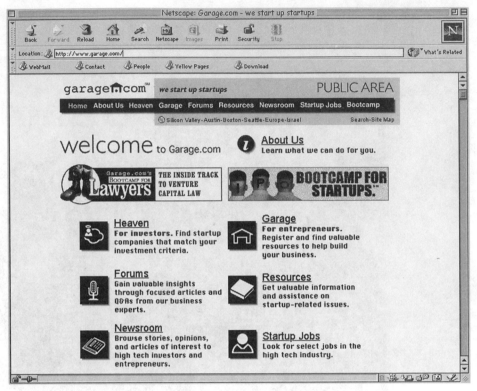

Figure 10. Does your elevator pitch need a tune-up? If so, it's time for a visit to this garage.

- A good general resource on everything from individual VC firms to conferences and Web sites is hidden within Yahoo's new corporate financing area:

  http://dir.yahoo.com/Business_and_Economy/Companies/Financial _Services/Financing/Corporate_Finance/Venture_Capital/

LEXICON/VOCABULARY/ARGOT/E-BIZ SLANG/A-VIRTUAL-ROSE-BY-ANY-OTHER-NAME GLOSSARY

This dot-com section will help you schmooze with the angels. Want to polish your elevator pitch and avoid kludges? Then prepare yourself to delve into the depths of vortals and other virtual wonders!

Note: If distinguishing a bit from a byte seems trite to you, then skip the computer terminology section. Perchance, however, you're not so well-versed on your pro formas and/or branding? Then keep reading.

Of Emoticons and Acronyms

Life in the dot-com lane inevitably means many encounters of the e mail/IRC/chat/messaging kind. And if you don't know your LOL from your OTOH, you might as well stay in IRL ;-)

The good folks in cyberland have created a variety of Web sites documenting the numerous keyboard characters and acronyms that are used as shortcuts for everything from winking to whining online.

Here are my favorites:

- Visit mIRC - Emoticons for a list of both acronyms and emoticons:

  http://www.mirc.co.uk/emote.html

- At the Smileys and Emoticons for Effective Communication Web site, you'll find links to different categories of expressions, such as "Affirming, Supportive" and "Unhappy, Sad":

  http://www.windweaver.com/emoticon.htm

- In a bad mood? Visit the Smiley Dictionary to cheer yourself—and your e-mail correspondents:

  http://www.netsurf.org/~violet/Smileys/

- An unabbreviated array of computer-related acronyms and abbreviations awaits you at BABEL:

  http://www.access.digex.net/~ikind/babel.html

- You'll find a short list of the most commonly used acronyms and emoticons in the E-mail Glossary:

  http://everythingemail.net/email_glossary.html

Let's Talk about Tunneling and Trojan Horses

Sometimes it seems as if the techie world concocts a word-a-day—and staying au courant with the latest buzz term can be mighty difficult. Luckily, a variety of Web sites have sprung up to help you chat with even the techiest of techies.

- Whatis.com is one of my favorites (Figure 11). You'll find definitions, references, and general Internet information:

  http://www.whatis.com/

- Webopedia's thorough computer dictionary covers an extensive array of Internet terminology and other computertese:

  http://www.pcwebopaedia.com/

- CMP's TechEncyclopedia contains a fast search engine, plus links to a variety of online computer magazines:

  http://www.techweb.com/encyclopedia/

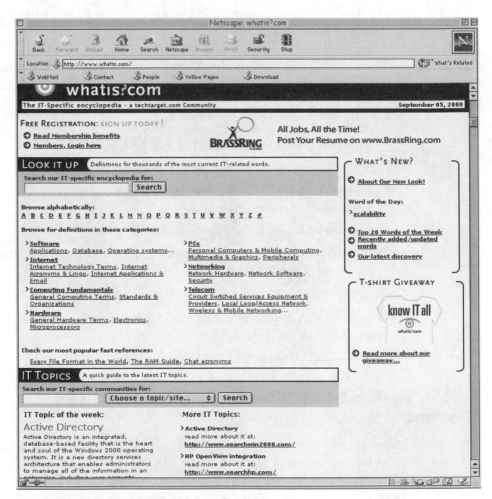

Figure 11. What is whatis? Click here for the answer.

Move into Managing and Marketing Mode

- The Management and Technology Dictionary includes everything from Baby Bells to Balance Sheets and beyond:

  http://www.euro.net/innovation/Management_Base/Mantec.Dictionary.html

- The Virtual Consultant, courtesy of *Inc.* magazine, has created a nifty searchable database of marketing terminology:

  http://www.inc.com/virtualconsult/databases/marketing_terms.html

- Although it's labeled as just for investors, general business terms are nicely defined at FinancialWeb University:

  http://www.financialweb.com/fwuniversity/

A Word a Day Keeps the Buzz Doctor Away

One of my new favorite terms is "vortual" (defined by some as a "vertical portal," regarded by others as an excellent example of useless terminology that someone probably spent hours concocting). Ours is not to judge—but to stay au courant.

With that in mind, here are my recommendations for keeping your marketing-e-commerce-dot-com slang up to date:

- The San Jose Mercury News is the place to go for the latest Silicon Valley news and notes. Among its features is this clever venture capital glossary:

  http://www3.mercurycenter.com/business/center/vcquiz/html/vocabq.htm

- Get hip to the latest happenings with *Fast Company* magazine, which focuses on the new paradigms (there's a good buzz word for you) of business:

  http://www.fastcompany.com/homepage/

- And *Business 2.0* will also put you in the fast lane—the magazine's an excellent way to keep up with the e-commerce world, and I particularly recommend the "New Economy Portal" section of the site for everything from links to other magazines with the latest dot-com and biz news (try Red Herring, for example) to places to go for marketing research, financial tools, media bits & bytes, and more:

  http://www.business2.com/services/n_e_p.html

MARKETING AND ADVERTISING: SHOW ME THE CUSTOMERS!

You can have the most beautifully designed site on the Web, the penultimate fabulous product or service, and the best employees in the galaxy. But if you think you'll save money if you skip the marketing and advertising side of your e-biz, I've got some bad news: you just flunked E-biz 101.

The good news: you don't have to spend excessive amounts of pre-sales dollars to start a solid marketing and ad campaign. And these Web sites can help show you how:

- *Entrepreneur* magazine's dot-com site has an extensive section guiding you through the sales, marketing, and advertising process. Included are articles, virtual workshops, and relevant links:

  http://www.entrepreneurmag.com/marketing/

- Tracking your target market, reading the results of surveys about customer responses and needs, learning to understand marketing statistics…these components of marketing are also essential as you expand your e-biz. Numerous Web sites are devoted to the area of market research—here are some of the best:

  - Nua Internet Surveys is an excellent source of international information, and you can subscribe to a free newsletter at the site:

    http://www.nua.ie/surveys/index.cgi

  - ACNielson offers extensive market research and statistics, and the site is updated frequently with the results of the company's latest studies:

    http://www.acnielsen.com/

  - CyberAtlas focuses on Internet statistics specifically for online marketers, and I recommend signing up for their free weekly newsletter to stay atop of their research:

    http://cyberatlas.internet.com/

  - Jupiter Communications features market research about online consumers. You will have to register to read some of the material:

    http://www.jup.com/

- If you're in the B2B (business-to-business) biz, or just want to check on your competition, Hoover's Online is the hot spot. You can also sign up for a free newsletter at the site:

  http://www.hoovers.com/

- For general Internet marketing news, add Internet.com's Marketing Channel to your list of favorites. You'll find not only the latest news, but links to a wealth of free online resources:

  http://www.internet.com/sections/marketing.html

- DoubleClick's special learning center contains resources on advertising, site promotion, market research, and other related topics:

  http://www.doubleclick.net/learning_center/online_resources/

- The always excellent Inc. Online comes through again for entrepreneurs wanting marketing and advertising assistance. The guide to doing business online includes a variety of helpful articles about the marketing/advertising side of e-biz:

  http://www.inc.com/internet/articles/tutorials/

- The name of this site may make you smile—but Guerilla Marketing Online has a lot of bite behind its King-Kong buzz. Although you do have to pay for some of the products advertised here, there are numerous free resources (including some helpful marketing-related articles) available. I recommend starting with the "Weekly Guerilla" in the Tactics section:

  http://www.gmarketing.com/tactics/weekly.html

- Ad Resource offers a treasure chest of Web site promotion resources and information about the how-tos of Internet advertising. There's a primer to get you going, a glossary to teach you those marketing buzz words like *click-through* and *opt-in e-mail*, and a sample rates section that you can use as a guide for advertising:

  http://adres.internet.com/

- LinkExchange sounds like a site for golfers. Well, you're overlooking a golden tee if you skip this URL for that reason. Its resources range from a Banner Network to methods for tracking site visits, creating a privacy policy for your customers, and more:

  http://www.linkexchange.com/

- Make sure that your site can be easily located through search engines and directories. Some sites, such as Yahoo!, have sections where you can submit your link; alternatively, you can use a variety of online submission services to submit your site automatically, or select software that lets you submit your site automatically. You can find a list of options, such as Submit It! (http://www.submit-it.com/), at Instantweb.com:

  http://www.instantweb.com/help/sites/webhelp.html#publicize

- The Federal Trade Commission's section on Advertising Policy Statements and Guidance may sound a tad boring (Figure 12). But don't let the long name stop you from visiting this site. The articles are well-written and detailed; I particularly recommend the Frequently Asked Advertising Questions from small business owners:

  http://www.ftc.gov/bcp/guides/guides.htm

- Promotion 101 has more than a clever name. This nicely designed site contains a variety of excellent articles and tools to help you with marketing and promoting your site:

  http://www.promotion101.com/

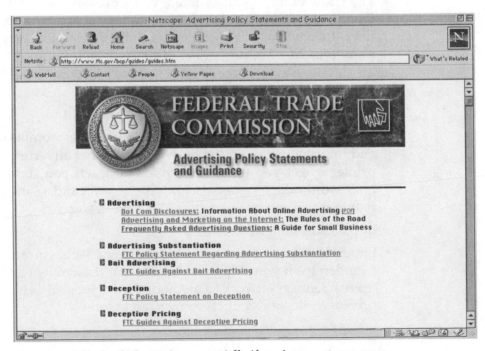

Figure 12. Just the FAQs, ma'am, especially if you're an entrepreneur.

CUSTOMER SERVICE...DO IT WITH A SMILE

Here's one area that is similar in the real world: you need to satisfy your customer. Otherwise, all your efforts might as well have been devoted to coming up with a grand scheme for winning the lottery.

Surveys show that online customer complaints range from the lack of personal service ("I kept trying to find a phone number or someone, but all I could find were a bunch of Web pages!" my friend Dorothy recently complained after she had abandoned her virtual shopping cart halfway through a purchase at a natural foods e-shoppe) to requests for personal information without details about what will be done with the data (I clicked File | Close in my Web browser window after almost completing a purchase of a toy for my nephew when a site demanded my social security number—and I couldn't find a privacy statement or any information about what the site did with the information that I provided).

The U.S. Small Business Administration believes customer service and quality "may well be the biggest competitive weapon of the 20th century and beyond." Customers who don't receive the service that they want before, during, and after their purchase take their business elsewhere either before or after the sale. And they often spread the word.

Losing a customer is expensive. The SBA cites studies showing that 91 percent of unhappy customers will never buy again from a company that has displeased them — and they express their dissatisfaction to at least seven other people.

"The bottom line in customer service is that it's only as good as the customer says it is. When employees start focusing on how to better meet the needs of their customers, they become more sensitive to the processes they perform and how to improve and/or change them to achieve the results the customer desires," the SBA advises. And the administration calls customer service "the imperative of the 1990s."

"Consumers are beginning to feel that their needs haven't been met," explains Bonnie Jansen of the U.S. Office of Consumer Affairs. "They're sick of getting poor service all the time."

The National Federation of Independent Business (NFIB) in Washington, D.C. recently released the results of a three-year study showing that small businesses emphasizing quality customer service were more likely to succeed than competitors who put the emphasis on lowering prices or providing a special type of product.

So how do you serve the customer?

The SBA offers these "golden rules":

Golden Rule #1: Put the Customer First. Make your employees aware that this customer-focused service is essential and set standards.

Golden Rule #2: Stay Close to Your Customers. Set up a customer service system that provides details on how the customer can get in touch with a real person. In addition, place an easily completed form on the site that allows customers to send in their feedback. Then train your employees (and yourself!) to ask questions and listen to the responses. Change your e-biz to suit your customer, and ask for suggestions from not only your customers but your employees, external services, and any brutally honest friends.

The Customer Service Institute's research shows that 65 percent of a company's business comes from existing customers, and that it costs five times as much to attract a new customer than to keep an existing one satisfied.

Golden Rule #3: Pay Attention to the Little Details. From answering customers' queries promptly (for example, answering the phone on the third ring, responding to e-mails within a few days) to communicating respectfully to following up a customer's purchase with a note of appreciation, it's the little things that count.

In addition to these considerations, dot-com customer service involves some special challenges, from purchasing paths to payment policies. Here are some sites to help you meet those challenges:

- *Windows* magazine recently published an extensive feature on e-commerce. Pay particular attention to the links focusing on customers, such as customer relations:

   http://www.winmag.com/library/1999/0801/fea0057.htm

- There are a variety of software solutions, although most experts advise that you combine software customer service with some form of "real person" service as an option. One of the more interesting options is LivePerson (http://www.liveperson.com/), which lets the customer chat with a representative. For a listing of your options, see:

   http://dir.yahoo.com/Business_and_Economy/Companies/Corporate _Services/Customer_Service/Software/

- Put yourself in the customer's mind. What do you want when you're shopping online? An excellent first step is to read the FTC's "Shop

Safely" document—and consider how you can make your customer feel that the shopping is "safe" on your site:

http://www.ftc.gov/bcp/conline/pubs/online/cybrsmrt.htm

The FTC also publishes a guide for online businesses about the delivery end of customers' purchases:

http://www.ftc.gov/bcp/conline/pubs/alerts/intbalrt.htm

- For more details on these and related topics, check out the SBA's Small Business Success Series (Figure 13):

http://www.sba.gov/gopher/Business-Development/Success-Series/

NO LAWYER JOKES, PLEASE: YOU NEVER KNOW WHEN YOU'LL NEED ONE

Set aside your collection of legal humor, and recognize the facts: much of real-world and virtual-reality business revolves around legalese. Even if you're not contemplating incorporating or an IPO, your dot-com biz will involve checking out and obeying federal, state, and local laws governing business. And then, of course, there's always the IRS…

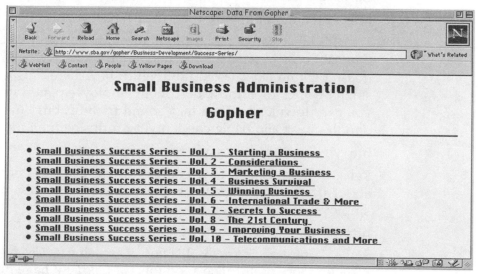

Figure 13. Although it's basic, the SBA's Success Series offers a clear and concise overview of business plan components.

And so, let's talk of taxes and torts:

- The Business Law Site is an excellent resource for both specific (for example, trademark and copyright law) and general (e.g., legal checklists and forms) legal issues:

  http://members.aol.com/bmethven/index.html

- The Law News Network is worth repeated visits: it contains daily updates. If you like what you see, you can sign up for a free newsletter as well. And don't overlook the IPO Watch link, which reveals which law firms are handling different offerings. There are also links to EDGAR Online and SEC filings search engines.

  http://www.lawnewsnetwork.com/

- Want a synonym for "confusing"? I nominate "Internet taxation." Fortunately, there's a Web site that features an Internet tax table and individual state summaries of Internet taxation laws:

  http://www.vertexinc.com/taxcybrary20/CyberTax_Channel/tax-channel_70.html

- Tax matters can be, well, taxing. But Deloitte & Touche's Web site contains an online publication, Taxation in North America, that can help clarify this topic:

  http://www.dtonline.com/northamr/nacover.htm

- The IRS has created a Tax Information for Business Web site that is (honest!) easy to navigate, written in a friendly style, and, well, sure doesn't sound like the old IRS (Figure 14). There's a special area for small businesses, information about employee plans, and forms that you can download. (They may sound friendly, but I'm still going to double-check and triple-check my tax forms before I file...):

  http://www.irs.ustreas.gov/bus_info/

- Relax in the Business Law Lounge, where you can find information about everything from trusts to business structures to employer/employee issues to, well, trust me: it's worth a visit:

  http://www.lectlaw.com/bus.html

- Smile! You're on *Court TV*. It's not as amusing as *Candid Camera*, but it's a lot more useful. The good folks at *Court TV* have put together a Small Business Law Center that includes some useful links:

  http://www.courttv.com/legalhelp/business/

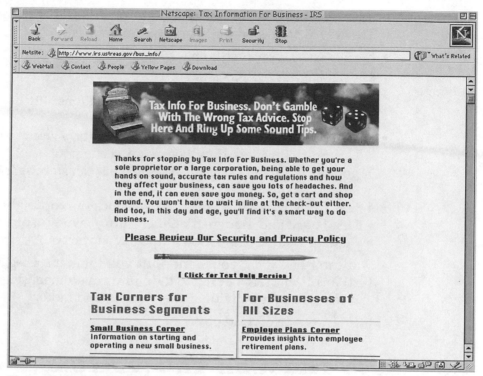

Figure 14. This might sound like an oxymoron, but trust me: it's a friendly, comprehensible IRS—at least the Internet version is.

- Employment law is one of the subjects that you may not think much about – until it affects you. With that in mind, check out DiscriminationAttorney.com:

  http://www.discriminationattorney.com/

- "Law for all" is their motto, and Nolo.com's Small Business Law section includes a variety of essential topics, such as small business legal structures and small business tax concerns:

  http://www.nolo.com/encyclopedia/sb_ency.html

- Findlaw.com contains both subject directories and a solid, fast search engine. You can hunt for the latest laws, codes, and more:

  http://www.findlaw.com/

- Another legal portal is the Cyberlaw Encyclopedia. Links include both Canadian and American high-tech and e-commerce legal topics:

  http://www.gahtan.com/cyberlaw/

- Interested in IPOs? There are a number of sites that cover this topic. The IPO Maven is both fast and well-organized:

  http://www.ipomaven.com/

- More help from Uncle Sam:
  - U.S. Business Advisor: laws and regulations: http://www.business.gov/busadv/maincat.cfm?catid=21
  - U.S. Securities Exchange Commission: http://www.sec.gov/
  - U.S. Small Business Handbook's tax section: gopher://gopher.gsa.gov/ 00/staff/pa/cic/smbuss/other/smallbus.txt
  - U.S. Copyright Office: http://lcweb.loc.gov/copyright/
  - U.S. Patent and Trademark Office: http://www.uspto.gov/
  - Federal Trade Commission: http://www.ftc.gov/

- Still can't find what you want—but you think it's a legal issue? Try FedWorld, which is a portal to the entire government (Figure 15). You can search for an individual site, reports, and more:

  http://www.fedworld.gov/

BREAKING THROUGH THE (VIRTUAL) GLASS CEILING: SITES FOR FEMALE ENTREPRENEURS

Networking takes on new meaning when women are involved. An increasing number of women are becoming entrepreneurs—and helping each other through formal and informal organizations. From the government to private industry, help for would-be and current female entrepreneurs is growing as well:

- The Forum for Women Entrepreneurs contains resources ranging from job listings to business planning help to articles to women-focused venture funds:

  http://www.fwe.org

- Want to know your options for starting your business on a shoestring budget? Putting together a wardrobe for a business trip and not sure what's appropriate? Click on over to Women's Wire Small Business area, where female entrepreneurs are the name of the game.

  womenswire.com/smallbiz/start/

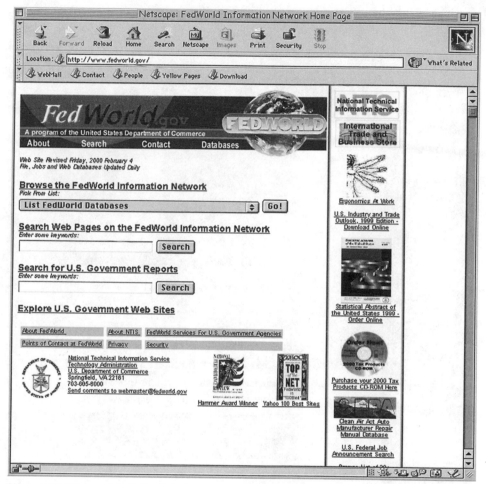

Figure 15. The world of the feds is yours to browse.

- The Online Women's Business Center offers interactive business training for female entrepreneurs, resources such as links to SBA women's business centers, an information exchange, and more (Figure 16):

    http://www.onlinewbc.org/

- The SBA's Office of Women's Business Ownership includes a detailed resource guide, links to networking groups, and help on business issues such as financing:

    http://www.sba.gov/womeninbusiness/index.html

Figure 16. News and networking opportunities abound at Office of Women's Business Ownership.

- WomenConnect.com is an excellent general resource for women in business, covering not only business topics, but related issues such as health:

  http://www.womenconnect.com/

- *Working Woman* magazine frequently features entrepreneurs in their articles. The Web site contains some excellent features such as a message board and a variety of databases:

  http://www.workingwomanmag.com/

- This association for female executives offers resources, networking, events, and services. There is a cost to join, but it's relatively low (as of this writing, it was $29 annually):

  http://www.nafe.com/

YOUNG AT HEART—AND AGE: WEB SITES FOR YOUNG ENTREPRENEURS

Forget about being born with a silver spoon in your mouth. The really fortunate kids today are born with an Internet connection. Think I'm joking? I volunteered to babysit for a three-year-old last weekend.

"What do you want to do this afternoon, Taylor?" I asked him. I anticipated a response such as "go to the park," "watch TV," or, perhaps, "go to the pet store."

Instead, he skipped confidently over to the computer, patted it affectionately, and said sweetly, "Turn on and go to the Rugrats (http://www.nick.com/rugrats/noflash.html), and then go to Sesame Street (http://www.ctw.org/)."

I obeyed. On my next visit, Taylor will probably be talking about "pinging" and scolding me for bad netiquette.

If you have children and want to encourage them to become entrepreneurs, this next section can help.

In addition, if you're in high school or college, or a recent college graduate, the second section offers resources just for you.

Not for Kids Only

- The U.S. Patent and Trademark has a special section just for kids (Figure 17). It includes games, puzzles, contests, and more. Click the Guiding Lights link for resources for parents, teachers, and coaches:

  http://www.uspto.gov/web/offices/ac/ahrpa/opa/kids/index.html

- BizWorld was created to set up a program involving volunteers "teaching kids about business." It began when Northern Californian venture capitalist Tim Draper wanted to teach his daughter's class about the wondrous world of entrepreneurship and business. And it grew from there:

  http://www.bizworld.org/

Figure 17. Think you've got a budding entrepreneur? Click here for some inspiration.

- Junior Achievement involves more than 3 million students across the United States, and its goal by 2005 is to involve 20 percent of the student population (a total of 11 million students). The group describes its mission as ensuring "that every child in America has a fundamental understanding of the free enterprise system":

  http://www.ja.org/

- "I did it myyyyyy way!"—or the Kids Way, anyway. KidsWay Inc. teaches young people about the joys of becoming an entrepreneur.

There's a Young Entrepreneur Club, a newsmagazine, and separate areas just for kids, parents, and teachers:

http://www.kidsway.com/

- The National Foundation for Teaching Entrepreneurship describes itself as "an international nonprofit organization that introduces low-income teens from local communities to the world of business and entrepreneurship by teaching them how to develop and operate their own legitimate small businesses." There are a variety of components to this international organization, all focused on teaching young people:

http://www.nfte.com/

For Young Entrepreneurs

- The Umbrella Project has a variety of resources for young entrepreneurs. You'll find e-mail discussions, interviews, a job board, and an excellent library of links:

http://www.umbrellaproject.com

- Xtra, xtra! You can read all about small business as it relates to Generation X at the GenX Startup Web site. The writing style is light-hearted—but nestled amid the fun and games is a lot of useful information:

http://www.xstartup.com

IT'S BACK TO SCHOOL TIME: COLLEGES AND UNIVERSITIES WITH E-BIZ AIDS

Want some educated help with your e-biz efforts? Many colleges and universities offer Web pages that can be accessed by the public—and can assist you in improving your dot-com business. You won't have to memorize the school song or eat stale popcorn at the football rally to take advantage of these useful higher education sites:

- The University of California at Berkeley's Haas School of Business houses several centers that merge academic interests with high-tech corporate resources. In particular, check out the resources at the Center for Marketing and Technology and the Center for Entrepreneurship & Innovation:

http://haas.berkeley.edu/Research/research.html

- The ivy-woven walls of Harvard University include a business school (HBS) that includes some not-for-East-Coasters-only resources. A recent article in the online business review, for example, was entitled: "Bringing Silicon Valley Inside" (http://www.hbsp.harvard.edu/products/hbr/sepoct99/99504.html):

  http://www.hbs.harvard.edu/

- MIT's Sloan School of Management is one of the most well-known—and deservedly so. I recommend the Research Center and Business Publication links in particular:

  http://mitsloan.mit.edu/

- The Graziadio Business Report from Pepperdine University's School of Business and Management offers some interesting articles, both practical and theoretical, on a variety of business topics:

  http://bschool.pepperdine.edu/gbr/index.html

- UCLA's Graduate School of Business includes the Harold Price Center for Entrepreneurial Studies. Click Entrepreneurial Links to uncover a variety of extremely useful resources, ranging from finance to business publications to business foundations:

  http://www.anderson.ucla.edu/research/esc/

- Princeton University is home to a Survey Research Center that's a treasure chest of resources for those interested in marketing issues:

  http://www.princeton.edu/~abelson/index.html

- The venerable Vanderbilt University created Project 2000 to "study the marketing implications of commercializing the World Wide Web." The original project has grown into an outstanding research center for e-commerce, and the entrepreneur- and e-commerce-related links are excellent:

  http://ecommerce.vanderbilt.edu/

- Ohio State's Virtual Finance Library is much more than an academic resource tool. Entrepreneurs, investors, and others interested in various aspects of the financial world (both virtual and real) will find a wealth of resources here:

  http://www.cob.ohio-state.edu/dept/fin/overview.htm

- New York State University's Small Business Development Center includes a Research Network rich with links ranging from Internet commerce to marketing to startup info:

http://www.smallbiz.suny.edu/Research_Network/research_network.html

- To visit other business education Web sites, visit:

http://www3.mgmt.purdue.edu/bused_us.html

BITS & BYTES

This directory lists a sampling of the other types of resources available. These resources range from newsgroups to associations to portals, and the ones that you choose will, in general, depend on the type of product or service that you sell.

Newsgroups, Mailing Lists, and Chats

- Lizst is the mailing list directory of choice. Read the introduction if you're not familiar with joining and participating in mailing lists, and then use the search engine or find a list of interest to you by using the category directory:

http://www.liszt.com

- Use DejaNews to search through newsgroups and find ones of interest to you:

http://www.deja.com

- Chat sessions are becoming increasingly popular. A good place to learn about chatting is NetGuide's Internet Reference section. See the article on "Ways to Chat" and IRC:

http://www.netguide.com/Internet/Reference

- The Library of Congress has an excellent article on newsgroups, with links to relevant information (Figure 18):

http://lcweb.loc.gov/local/guides/news.html

- Yahoo! offers chat sessions on a variety of topics, and its help pages on participating in chats make it easy to get started:

http://chat.yahoo.com/chat/help/

- An increasingly popular place to hunt for e-mail lists is Onelist. You can quickly and easily join several lists at this site, and/or even start your own mailing list:

http://www.onelist.com

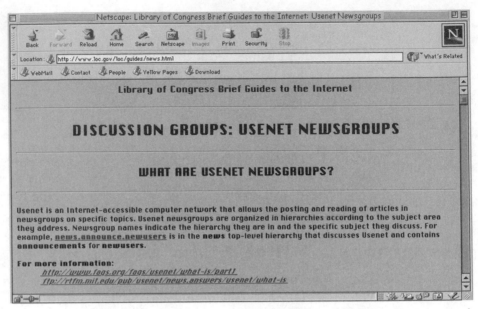

Figure 18. Want to see if you can find what you need on a newsgroup? The Library of Congress's article and links can lead the way.

- The U.S. government also has a good tutorial on mailing lists that incorporates links to other resources (Figure 19):

  http://www-ed.fnal.gov/linc/fall95/comm_lists/comm_list_home.html

Sign Up Here: Associations and Organizations

- Associations and organizations offer an excellent opportunity for net-working, learning more about your particular area of interest (for example, if you're offering online career counseling, you might consider joining a career counselor's group), and, as your business grows, finding partners and/or additional staff. The Gateway to Association at the American Society of Association Executives is a good resource for finding the right association for your needs:

  http://www.asaenet.org/Gateway/GatewayHP.html

- For a list of associations specifically for small businesses, visit SmallOffice.com's list of links:

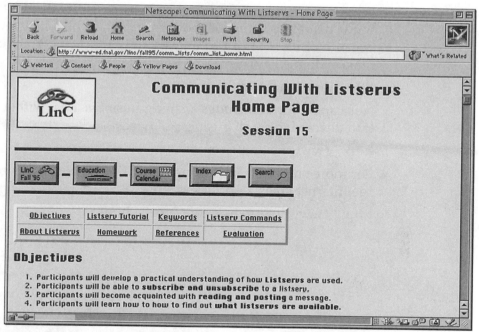

Figure 19. How do mailing lists function, and where can you find out more? If those are your questions, this article will provide the answers.

http://www.smalloffice.com/maven/sba.sba.htm

- Two well-known resources for entrepreneurs are:
  - the National Alliance of Business: http://www.nab.com
  - and The National Association for the Self-Employed: http://www.nase.org

Portals and Partnerships

You often read references to the "portal wars" and the "buzz on the next portentous partnership." Well, the portal battles aren't over—but they are worth tracking. In addition to offering useful resources, they often offer opportunities for those interested in partnerships.

Some of the most recently in-the-news portals include:

- Go2Net, which includes among its features the HyperMart, with free Web housing for business:

  http://www.go2net.com/index.html

- What can you say about AOL? Well, some folks love it; others hate it, but it definitely is one of those portals that folks like my mom love because of its ease of use and friendly touches ("You've got mail!" makes Mom's day):

  http://www.aol.com

- Netscape's portal includes a strong business area, with a special section devoted to small businesses' needs:

  http://www.netscape.com

- For more on portals, including how to create one for your own e-biz, see Internet Week's portal section:

  http://www.internetwk.com/portal.htm

Index